P9-AOG-880

The Love of Izayoi & Seishin

A Kabuki Play by Kawatake Mokuami

THE LOVE OF
IZAYOI & SEISHIN

Translated by Frank T. Motofuji

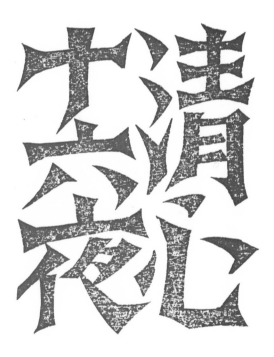

Charles E. Tuttle Co.
RUTLAND, VERMONT & TOKYO, JAPAN

HARVARD-YENCHING LIBRARY
HARVARD UNIVERSITY
2 DIVINITY AVENUE

Publisher

JUN 1 3 1969

W5915.8/43

Representatives

For Continental Europe:
BOXER BOOKS INC., Zurich
For the British Isles:
PRENTICE-HALL INTERNATIONAL INC., London
For Australasia:
PAUL FLESCH & CO., PTY. LTD., Melbourne

Published by the Charles E. Tuttle Company Inc.
of Rutland, Vermont & Tokyo, Japan

with editorial offices at
Suido 1-chome, 2-6, Bunkyo-ku, Tokyo, Japan

Copyright in Japan, 1966
by Charles E. Tuttle Co., Inc.

All rights reserved
Library of Congress Catalog Card No. 66-16266
First printing 1966

Book design and typography by John Paull
PRINTED IN JAPAN

PL 810 .A9 K63

Kawatake, Mokuami, 1816-
  1893.

Love of Izayoi & Seishin

Dedicated to
DENZEL CARR

CONTENTS

INTRODUCTION

KAWATAKE MOKUAMI (1816–1893) was the last great playwright for the kabuki, the popular theater. He is credited with close to four hundred pieces, making him the most prolific writer in the history of the Japanese theater. Even discounting the fact that many of them were adaptations from older plays and that he had numerous disciples during his productive years to help him write the less important scenes, this is a staggering accomplishment. His plays are frequently given today, and *The Love of Izayoi and Seishin* is one of the most popular.

Mokuami's real name was Yoshimura Yoshisaburō. He was born in Edo (later Tokyo), where his family had lived for five generations. We know nothing definite about his schooling, but since his father was a pawn-broker, the boy must have been sent to a temple school for a rudimentary education, as he later kept the books. When he was sixteen, Mokuami was hired as a delivery boy by a book dealer. He became familiar with various types of popular literature, including the texts of puppet and kabuki plays, and errands frequently took him back-stage into the three licensed kabuki theaters of Edo.

When Mokuami was eighteen, his father died. As the

eldest son, he had to manage the business, but being temperamentally unsuited for it he turned it over to his younger brother. He then drifted about until a dance teacher suggested that he become an apprentice to a playwright, a relative of hers. He took her advice and in 1835 became a disciple of Tsuruya Magotarō (1796–1852). Magotarō, who was not an especially gifted writer, was the adopted grandson of Tsuruya Namboku IV (1755–1829), the outstanding playwright before Mokuami.

Apprentice playwrights in the Edo period did not begin their training by writing. They were not much more than servants at the beginning. They then moved up to the position of scribe, excerpting and copying the dialogue of each character in a play for the actors assigned the roles, and making final copies of scripts. They were also expected to make preliminary sketches for theater billboards and handbills and to conduct preliminary rehearsals of minor scenes for the playwright, who was responsible for the staging of all his plays. If the apprentice carried out his duties satisfactorily, he was finally given the task of writing a scene under the supervision of the playwright. In 1840, after seven years with Magotarō, Mokuami was assigned an entire act.

In 1841 the three official theaters were ordered by the government to relocate in the outlying Asakusa district. This was part of a program of curbing extravagance among the townsmen and improving the moral climate. Mokuami became the chief playwright of one of the theaters and took the name of Kawatake Shinshichi II. (The first Shinshichi, who was active toward the end of the eighteenth century, produced little of importance.) In the following ten years, Mokuami did not distinguish himself in any way. This was due in part to the conservative policy of the management which favored the old (and mainly history) plays to original domestic dramas, which were Mokuami's forte. The first original domestic

play by Mokuami was produced in 1851. It was an unexpected success, and the delighted management gave
him opportunities to write more. But it was not until 1854
that he finally came into his own.

In that year the actor Ichikawa Kodanji IV (1812–1866)
came from Osaka for the season. This was the actor for
whom Mokuami wrote his most famous plays, and the
association was to last until the actor's death. Kodanji
was not of distinguished lineage (pedigree is important in
the kabuki). He was unimpressive physically and vocally,
and although he had a wide range of roles (leading man,
villain, female parts, and could dance), he was not noted
for his dramatic ability until he worked with Mokuami,
who also profited by the association. He preferred writing
original plays involving thieves and other criminals, and
in Kodanji he found his ideal interpreter. They collabo-
rated on twenty-six domestic plays and five history plays.
Kodanji's death left the Edo theater bereft of its star
performer, but waiting in the wings were the young actors
who were to become the leading figures in the kabuki of
the Meiji era: Ichikawa Danjūrō IX (1838–1903), Onoe
Kikugorō V (1844–1903), and Ichikawa Sadanji (1842–
1904). Mokuami was to write for all of them.

The Tokugawa shogunate came to a turbulent end
when Mokuami was in his prime. But because the kabuki
was shackled by the regulation which prohibited depiction
of any person or event of the Tokugawa period, almost
none of the momentous events and changes confronting
the nation was reflected in the traditional theater. It was
left to the new drama from 1880 to come to grips with
important political and social problems.

This is not to say that some minor internal reforms and
external physical changes did not affect the kabuki.
Theaters were built along western architectural lines; box-
offices replaced theater teahouses as purveyors of tickets;
and gaslight was installed. Writers from outside infil-

trated the kabuki with cries for reform. They had returned
from abroad and were eager to remodel the kabuki in the
western image. They advocated elimination of the erotic
and vulgar, and insisted on the substitution of antiquarian
authenticity for the numerous historical inaccuracies in
the plays. Mokuami, as the leading playwright of the day,
was their pet scapegoat. The prospectus of the Society for
the Reformation of the Drama, which was issued in 1886,
read in part, "... we believe that the ugliness or beauty of
a play depends to a large extent upon the skill of the
writer. Granting this, we observe not a single gentleman
of learning among our playwrights. They all attract the
lower classes merely by a facile patchwork of stale ideas."

Sensing the winds of change, Mokuami announced his
retirement, and in 1881, at the age of sixty-five, com-
pleted what he believed would be his last play. In it,
characteristically, all of the main characters were criminals. He gave the name of Kawatake Shinshichi to his
leading disciple and took the name Mokuami. This name
has a special significance. It comes from the expression
moto no Mokuami ("back to the old Mokuami") and
refers to a humble person who, like the original Mokuami, a blindman forced by circumstances to impersonate
a feudal lord, returns voluntarily to his former state. But
it was not possible for a writer of Mokuami's stature and
ability to retire completely. Theater owners and actors
persuaded him to continue writing.

Mokuami had been stung by the disparagement of the
critics. He now wrote plays, characterized by historical
accuracy, which were called "living history plays." They
were so real they expired out of sheer dullness. Mokuami
also wrote domestic plays with a contemporary back-
ground, but they were only superficially modern. The
male characters wore their hair in the new western style,
but in spirit they were similar to the characters in Mokuami's earlier plays. The theater-goers demanded plays

with scenes laid in the nostalgic past. It is with these that Mokuami achieved his greatest successes in the Meiji period. Kikugorō V, an actor whose style owed much to Kodanji IV, appeared in many of these. It was for him that Mokuami wrote his last piece before suffering the stroke that paralyzed his left side and led to his death on February 22, 1893. His death poem read:

> *In vain it has waited*
> *For the flowering spring:*
> *The old plum tree*
> *That withers from one branch.*

The Love of Izayoi and Seishin is a domestic play, or, more accurately, a sub-class in the domestic play. The three main classifications in kabuki drama are the history play, the domestic play, and the dance narrative. In the history play the characters are of the warrior class. The language is formal and the acting is stylized. In the domestic plays the characters are from the townsman class, mainly well-to-do merchants. Chikamatsu (1653–1725) originated this style for the puppet theater. The dialogue is in the vernacular and the acting is realistic. The subclass in the domestic play is the "raw" domestic play. This label derives from the fact that the plays are populated by characters from the lowest strata of the plebeian class. Namboku IV pioneered this style and Mokuami brought it to perfection. *The Love of Izayoi and Seishin* is typical of Mokuami's "raw" domestic plays. The plot revolves around a dishonored Buddhist monk turned thief, and a prostitute who casts her lot in with him.

The play was first given in 1859. It had a different title and was performed in seven acts. One of the conventions in the kabuki by this time was that a play had to be in several acts which alternated in the history-play and domestic-play styles. The second, fourth, sixth, and seventh acts of this play were in the "raw" domestic play style and proved to be more popular than the history acts. It is these four acts which make up the play popularly known as *The Love of Izayoi and Seishin*. It is not, however, a completely self-contained play. Occasional references are made to events in the history scenes, and in the last act a character from the history section appears. (For the sake of clarity, brief synopses of the omitted acts are given on page 21.)

The play had a great success, but because the two leading male characters were based on actual persons and insufficiently disguised, the censors demanded that deletions and revisions be made. A dissolute priest at the Kan'ei Temple in Ueno had suggested the character of Seishin to Mokuami. This priest, after numerous lapses in conduct, had turned thief and earned the name of Seikichi the Devil Priest. In 1806, at the age of twenty-eight, he was arrested in Kyoto, brought back to Edo, tried, and decapitated. Hakuren, the other leading character in the play, was modeled after the thief who broke into the shogun's treasury in 1855 and made off with 4000 gold coins. Mokuami was inconsistent in his observance of the regulation against too close historical verisimilitude. He used the conventional aliases (which fooled nobody in the audience): Kamakura stood for Edo; the Inase River for the Sumida; the Hanamizu Bridge for the Eitai or Ryogoku; Minamoto Yoritomo (1147–1199), the founder of the Kamakura shogunate, for Tokugawa Ieyasu (1542–1616); and Ōiso for the Yoshiwara. But Mokuami also mentions actual place names in Edo like Broad Avenue, which was near Ryogoku Bridge, and the Hundred Piles on the Sumida River. It was only after the fall of the Tokugawa government that this and other ordinances could safely be ignored and plays given as written.

The play exemplifies many of Mokuami's characteristics and style and embodies the philosophy which underlies most of his "raw" domestic plays. The theme is retribution. A series of events carries the action forward and illustrates this theme; a man's circumstances and all his acts are governed by the Buddhist law of karma, or the law of cause and effect. Since every cause has an effect and every effect a cause, a man's reward or punishment in this world has a direct relation to his deeds here and in a previous existence. Every act in this world is therefore preordained. This theme is reiterated at intervals throughout the play. The initial robbery is justified by Seishin on the grounds that it was the victim's predestined misfortune to be at a particular place at a particular time, carrying a substantial sum of money. Seishin sees his own suicide at the end of the play as having been predetermined. This tenet in popular Buddhism was an important part of the mental baggage of the Edo townsman (as to some extent it still is of the modern Japanese), and was a valid theme for a play. The nature of this theme also explains what might be taken as lack of dramatic ingenuity, namely, the various coincidences which occur at crucial moments. (Seishin unknowingly is accessory to the death of his brother-in-law, and later unwittingly exposes his brother as a thief.) But these incidents are the dreadful tightening in the net of circumstances inexorably closing in on Seishin, and they are made more moving to Japanese audiences for their being beyond his control.

Implicit in the play was the didactic thesis of "promoting good and chastising evil." This edifying idea had been seized on by playwrights of the late seventeenth century to justify the existence of kabuki. At this time the theatre had become the target of the shogun's Confucian advisers, who looked upon the kabuki as being on a par with brothels as sources of immorality and extravagance. The dramatists had stilled criticism by promising to point up the moral that good always triumphed over evil. This was perhaps not so much the hindrance that it would seem to be at first glance. There was the other side of the coin: the most licentious scenes could be played and the most heinous crimes committed on stage so long as the criminals repented and paid for their deeds.

Among such crimes in Mokuami's "raw" domestic plays was murder. Namboku's murder scenes are brutal and savage, but the horror in Mokuami's bloody scenes is greatly ameliorated by the poetic language employed and by the use of music and stylized, almost choreographic, movements. (In this play, Motome dies of a self-inflicted injury, but Seishin believes himself to be the boy's murderer; he also causes the death of Izayoi.) Another crime–extortion figured so frequently in late Tokugawa domestic plays that the term "extortion scene" came into existence. (In the present play, it occurs at the beginning of Act VI where Seishin and Izayoi blackmail her former protector. Their scheme is successful but it ends with an ironic twist of fate: their victim is exposed as a thief and it is his long-lost brother who does this.) And so many robbers figure in Mokuami's plays that he was known as "the thieves' playwright."

Some remarks must be made about the language and stylistic devices used by Mokuami. In the scenes leading up to a climax the speeches are all in the vernacular. In the climactic scenes they are written in the consciously heightened form of poetry, and in classical Japanese this means the use of the basic pattern of alternating lines in five and seven syllables; the "pivot word," which runs together, with no hint of transition, two separate ideas; and "related words," which are words related to one another by class or quality and are woven into the text. An example of the pivot word is found in the opening line of the Kiyomoto lyrics in Act II, Scene 2: "Even on a hazy moonlit night the images of the stars number one, two, three, four, five. 'Five strokes on the alarm bell?'" (p. 24). The reckoning of the stars slips at the number "five" into the number of bell strokes which Izayoi fears is the alarm raised at the discovery of her flight. In this literary device the logical conclusion of the first part and the beginning of the second are left unexpressed. An example of the "related words" is found in Act II, Scene 4. Seishin begins by referring to the river on whose banks he and Motome have met. This then calls forth such words as "current," "ice," "freeze," and "waves." (p. 60.) Mokuami was also fond of splitting lines so that the thought expressed by the first character is carried on by a second (or third or fourth) and then tossed back to the first and brought to a conclusion (pp. 23–24, 38–39, 48–49, 60, 123).

These literary devices present problems of varying difficulty for the translator. The "split dialogue" and the "related words" are relatively easy. The pivot word, however, can only be translated literally in a clumsy way or explained in elaborate footnotes. When they occur in this play, the cunning effect has been sacrificed for the meaning. No attempt has been made to retain the syllabic count; this is an impossibility.

Another problem is the structure of the play. Western readers expecting a long sweep leading to a climax will be disappointed. As in most kabuki plays, there are several climaxes distributed in each act. The most important in this play occur as follows: Act II: the encounter of Izayoi and Seishin, Motome's death, and Seishin's metamorphosis in character; Act IV: Izayoi's renunciation of the world; Act VI: the extortion scene and the discovery of the fraternal relationship between Seishin and Hakuren; Act VII: Izayoi's death and Seishin's suicide. The structural balance is further upset by the almost equal importance of three characters—Seishin, Izayoi, and Hakuren. (In Act IV Seishin does not appear, and Hakuren is the leading character.) Moreover, too much is made of the haiku poet and his comic junkman friend in Act IV.

[17]

This can be explained by the fact that the kabuki has always been a repertory theater with a full complement of actors signed for the season. Once the company was assembled, it was the playwright's responsibility to provide each actor with roles within his specialty. (Actors specialized in the following parts: young man, adult male, villain, old man, adolescent boy, comic, young girl, adult woman, old woman, and child. In the 1859–1860 season there happened to be three senior actors and a popular comedian at the theater for which Mokuami was the house writer.) This necessity sometimes led Mokuami and others to write a big scene for each actor to play. A glaring example here is the death of Ofuji in Act VI. Hakuren's wife has been a secondary character until attention is suddenly focused upon her in a contrived and unbelievable scene. She pretends to turn informer on her husband after the revelation that he is a thief, in order to force her husband to kill her. It was a role tailored to the personality of an actor who specialized in playing noble women.

The use of music by Mokuami has been mentioned. He was partial to the Kiyomoto school for its pensive and melancholy melodic line which made it peculiarly suitable for sad love scenes. He used it in Act II, Scene 2, in the encounter of Izayoi and Seishin. (It must be noted here that the narrator, or chanter, and a samisen player accompany the scene in full sight of the audience. The chanter in other scenes of the play is normally concealed.) The lyrics for this scene were written by Mokuami, but he often appropriated them from other Kiyomoto pieces or from the narratives of puppet plays. In the latter case, Mokuami sets the scene so that the music comes from a neighboring house. This procedure is sometimes unsatisfactory. The emotional state of the actors onstage and the characters in the music may coincide in general, but not always in detail. In Act VII, Seishin's overwrought

condition as he prepares to kill his son is echoed in the
narration from a puppet play about a father's anguish
at the impending execution of his wayward daughter.
There is a concurrence in pathos, but the narrative is so
famous that it serves to distract rather than intensify the
tragic mood. But perhaps a similarity in mood was all
that Mokuami's audiences required, for in the face of the
overall impact of the scene, niceties of musical appropri-
ateness were of small import.

In treating the theme of retribution in terms of human
passions at a less-than-princely level, Mokuami was in
his element. The fate of a monk torn between the demands
of the flesh and the spirit, and the consequences of his
easy capitulation to worldly desires, were more readily
understandable to audiences than, say, the fate of an
ambitious warrior. They could also sympathize with a
prostitute more than with a princess. Monk and prostitute, bound by karma, lurk in the shadowy edge of
society, and even as they alter their course (he turns thief;
she becomes successively a kept woman, nun, wife and
mother), each new development brings them a step closer
to their ultimate destiny. Mokuami was aware of the
importance of contrasting moods in creating greater
dramatic force. Each of the four acts has a comic opening
which leads to one or more moving climaxes, some of
which are characterized by poetic passages of great
beauty. All of the leading roles are eminently playable—
another reason why this play, which is representative of
the works of one of the major playwrights in the kabuki,
and typical of a dramatic genre, has remained a favorite
in the kabuki repertory for over a hundred years.

SYNOPSIS OF
HISTORY PLAYS

ACT ONE

Koizuka Motome, Izayoi's brother and a page in the
Ōe household, is injured by a stray arrow during an
archery contest. Motome refuses monetary compensa-
tion, but when he learns that his father is trying desperately to raise an impossibly large sum, he accepts. Carrying the money, he starts home, unaware that it is meant
for Seishin, his sister's lover, whom he has never met.

Yaegaki Monza, a lordless samurai, is accepted as
retainer to the Ōe family on the recommendation of the
wicked advisor, Kageyama Budayū, who has seen evidence of Monza's skill with the sword and wishes to use
him for his own ends. Budayū binds Monza to him by
giving him a sword and the promise of his daughter's
hand in marriage.

ACT THREE

On the night of the wedding of his daughter to Monza,
Budayū reveals his plan of overthrowing the Ōe family
and demands that Monza join him. Monza is forced to
agree, but realizing that his loyalty to the Ōe family is

greater, he changes his mind, kills Budayū who turns on him, and escapes. Seishin, now a thief, has broken into Budayū's house to steal an heirloom sword, and observes Monza's flight. Monza is accused of the theft. It is this sword which Seishin restores to Budayu's son Shigenojō in Act VII, Scene 2.

ACT FIVE

Shigenojō tracks Monza down in the Hakone mountains and corners him. When Shigenojō tumbles over a cliff, Monza leaps after him, explains the reason for his murder of Budayū, and then commits suicide, bitterly regretting the unjust accusation of the theft of the sword. The reunion of Seishin and Izayoi in Hakone is effected in a conventional kabuki scene–a brief and wordless dumbshow.

TRANSLATOR'S NOTES

The translation is of the entire work as published in the collected works of Mokuami (*Mokuami Zenshū*, vol. 3, pp. 347–509). The only additions to the text have been supplementary stage directions (mainly the way certain lines were delivered), and a note on the time element for each act. These minor changes have been made for the sake of clarity.

In the stage directions the areas designated as "stage right," "stage left," "stage rear," etc., are in relation to the actor facing the audience.

All names except the author's on the title page are given in the Japanese manner: the family name first followed by the given name.

The Love of Izayoi & Seishin

ACT TWO

ACT FOUR

ACT SIX

ACT SEVEN

CAST OF CHARACTERS
(In order of appearance)

GONJI, *a minor servant*

DEMPACHI, *a minor servant*

ICHISUKE, *a footman*

KYŌGETSU, *a young novice and disciple of Seishin at Paradise Temple*

SAGOBEI, *Izayoi's father*

TŌJŪRŌ, *a magistrate; later disguised as Mokusuke, a manservant*

SEISHIN, *a sexton at Paradise Temple; later the thief Seikichi*

KANE, *a streetwalker*

IZAYOI, *a courtesan*

SANJI, *a boatman*

HAKUREN, *a moneylender; in reality the thief Ōdera Shōbei*

MOTOME, *Izayoi's brother; a page*

GINSHICHI, *a junk dealer*

HEMPUKU, *a haiku poet*

YONE, *maid to Izayoi*

OFUJI, *Hakuren's wife*

TORA, *maid to Ofuji*

NIHACHI, *Tora's father; a noodle vendor*

DONSHICHI, *Nihachi's friend*

[25]

KANROKU, *Nihachi's friend*

SUKIZŌ, *a gravedigger*

DORAICHI, *a buyer of personal effects from cemetery offices*

SHIGENOJŌ, *a samurai searching for a valuable sword stolen by Seikichi*

ACT TWO SCENE ONE

Time: New Year's; late afternoon.

> *The scene is the foot of the Hanamizu Bridge in Kamakura, At stage center is a stall twelve feet wide, spread with rush matting; a shop for New Year's decorations. Round wreaths of plaited straw hang from its eaves. At stage left is the foot of the bridge, and at stage right, a watchman's shack. A light-blue backdrop hangs at the rear of the stage.*
>
> *The curtain opens to drum and flute music. We see Ichisuke, a footman, wearing a crested cotton gown and carrying a sword. Over his shoulder he carries straw sandals strung on a pole. Two minor servants, Gonji and Dempachi, are gossiping.*

GONJI: Hey, Ichisuke, I hear that a Buddhist priest who broke his vow of chastity is going to be brought to the Hanamizu bridge today and exiled from the city.

DEMPACHI: So that's why they have set up that shed for

exposing criminals on Broad Avenue.

ICHISUKE: (*with a laugh*) You fool! That over there is a New Year's decoration stall they haven't removed yet.

GONJI: I was wondering why it had those round straw wreaths. So they are leftovers from the end of the year, eh?

DEMPACHI: This monk who broke his vow of chastity—which temple does he belong to?

ICHISUKE: Didn't you know? He is Seishin, the sexton at Paradise Temple. He became infatuated with Izayoi, the prostitute at the Ōgiya in Ōiso. The upshot is exile.

DEMPACHI: But even a monk or a pederast is after all a man, so there is no reason for them to dislike women.

GONJI: Come to think of it, Shinran, the founder of my faith, was very human. He permitted his priests to eat and to marry. Isn't it a blessed faith?

ICHISUKE: I haven't had a woman in a long time. I have to go around hawking toothpicks and straw sandals to buy wine to go with my fish salad.

DEMPACHI: Me, too. I haven't had a woman since last month.

GONJI: Anyway, why don't we go have a drink somewhere?

ICHISUKE: I would like to join you, as it has been a long time since I had any wine. But the fact is I don't have a copper on me.

DEMPACHI: Don't worry about that. You heard Gonji—he'll pay.

GONJI (*upset*): What? What makes you think I have any money? If I did I would go drink by myself.

ICHISUKE: Were you counting on Dempachi, then?

GONJI: No, I was counting on your straw sandals.

ICHISUKE: I can't afford to buy you drinks on these. These straw sandals are worth three hundred coppers and I put in a lot of time on them. I was planning on buying myself a small amount of wine for a nightcap and getting myself a street walker for a hundred coppers.

DEMPACHI: That's a fine how-do-you-do!

GONJI: Never mind—buy us a small bottle and we will take care of the rest.

ICHISUKE (*alarmed*): I don't like the sound of that.

DEMPACHI: Come along, now, and don't make such a fuss.

ICHISUKE (*dismayed*): Confound it! I've been trapped by scoundrels!

> *Dempachi drags Ichisuke off toward stage left in the direction of the bridge. Gonji follows. Then Sagobei, Izayoi's father, comes up the runway extending from the rear of the theatre to the stage. He holds the hand of the eleven-year-old acolyte Kyōgetsu, who is dressed in a gray robe and a short clerical apron. They stop on the runway.*

KYŌGETSU: Tell me, Sagobei, is the place they are bringing Seishin very far away?

SAGOBEI: No, no, it is not far. They will soon be bringing him to the foot of that bridge you see over there.

KYŌGETSU: Then let us wait for him over there.

SAGOBEI: Come along now, and take care you don't stumble.

> *They continue to the stage proper.*

SAGOBEI (*sadly*): When I asked at the watchman's shack back there just now, he told me that they would be

[29]

leading him by at any moment. I have not seen him since he went to prison. I expect he has lost weight. Where will he go from here? I thought of giving him some money so that he could at least put his affairs in order. But I have been unable to do so. There has been no word from my son whom I sent off to try and raise some money. So I am certain he has failed. Ah! It seems there is no money to be had in the world.

KYŌGETSU (*eagerly*): Here, Sagobei, I don't have much, but if you want coppers, I have some temple offerings with me.

> *From under the collar of his gown he withdraws some money wrapped in paper.*

SAGOBEI: Oh, no, no. I do not need anything now. Keep it and don't lose it. Well, now, they certainly ought to be leading him by soon.

> *He looks down the runway.*

SAGOBEI (*excitedly*): Speak of a person and there is his shadow, they say. Look, look, over there.

KYŌGETSU: Is Seishin coming?

SAGOBEI: Yes, he is. We might get rebuked if we get in the way. Let's make ourselves inconspicuous.

> *The two conceal themselves in the back of the watchman's shack at stage right. From offstage come the sound of a drum beating as at the hourly tattoo, and music in the style of Buddhist liturgies. Two footmen in iris-patterned skirts and carrying poles about six feet in length lead the procession up the runway. They are followed by Seishin, with a month's growth of hair on his normally shaven head. He is dressed in a light-blue gown,*

[30]

*and is bound with a rope held by two
policemen wearing short black robes. He
is followed by Terasawa Tōjūrō, an
official. His jacket is split in the back for
his two swords, and he is attended by two
lackeys carrying a round campaign hat
and a camp stool. They come straight to
the main stage where the policemen lay
out a straw mat at stage center.*

POLICEMEN (*gruffly*): Sit down!

> *Seishin squats on the mat. His captors
> stand by at the rear. Terasawa seats him-
> self on the camp stool at stage left.*

TŌJŪRŌ (*gravely*): Seishin, disciple to Kyōzen of Paradise
Temple!

SEISHIN: Aye!

> *He bows.*

TŌJŪRŌ: It was most reprehensible of you, a monk, to
have become involved with the prostitute named Izayoi
employed at the Ōgiya in the post town of Ōiso, and to
have recklessly spent gold and silver on wine and
sensual pleasures. You ought to have been punished,
but on exceptional clemency, you are hereby banished
from the valleys and the seven counties of Kamakura.

SEISHIN: Aye!

TŌJŪRŌ: Accept your sentence with gratitude!

SEISHIN (*humbly*): I was told that when an only son takes
the tonsure, nine generations of his family are born in
heaven. I shaved off my hair in order to pray for the
repose of the souls of my parents, and under the tutelage of my master Kyōzen, prayed diligently day and
night for the past twenty-five years. But I was still unable to free myself from the wheel of transmigration in

[31]

this world, strayed into carnal ways, and now receive sentence from on high. From this moment on I will revert to my original pure heart, for my heart has awakened to the truth for the first time. For the mercy by which a heavy sentence has been commuted to an order of exile, I am extremely grateful.

He bows.

TŌJŪRŌ: Untie him.

POLICEMEN: Aye!

They free Seishin.

TŌJŪRŌ (*gently*): Now, then, that completes my official business. I received instructions from old Kyōzen at Paradise Temple in reading Buddhist texts by rote. I am therefore as good as a fellow disciple of yours, and I do not consider you a stranger. But the facts are that a thief entered Paradise Temple a while back, stole the 3000 gold pieces offered to the temple by Lord Yoritomo, and we do not know the whereabouts of this thief. Suspicion fell upon you, and we once interrogated you. But your protestations of innocence held up, and you are being exiled specifically on the crime of having broken your vow of chastity. Your old master always praised you for your talents and intelligence. His teachings of twenty-five years have come to nothing. He must be sorely disappointed. Since you are still young, mend your ways, train yourself further, and wipe away this disgrace to your old teacher. Unless you do this, you will not be called a true priest.

SEISHIN (*touched*): I am grateful to you for your kind advice. For the present I will quit this locality. To regain my status as priest I will cheerfully reside in any rude temple and undergo training. Then I will see you again.

TōJŪRō: Then I will petition on high for the commutation of your sentence of exile from Kamakura, and we will happily meet again.

SEISHIN: Until then, may you be in good health.

TōJŪRō: I hope you will concentrate on your training.

SEISHIN: Thank you.

TōJŪRō: As my official duties are now done with, I will report to my superiors about this matter.

He rises.

SEISHIN: Goodbye, Terasawa.

TōJŪRō: Seishin, you must not linger.

SEISHIN: Aye!

He bows.

TōJŪRō: Attendants, come!

The hour-drum tattoo is played, and Tōjūrō leads his entourage down the runway. There is a commotion, and Sagobei and Kyōgetsu run in from stage right.

SAGOBEI (*joyfully*): Seishin, you are alive and well!

SAGOBEI and KYōGETSU: Our felicitations!

They embrace Seishin.

SEISHIN: Oh! You surprised me. You are Izayoi's father and Kyōgetsu the acolyte. I am grateful to you for coming to see me.

Melancholy music is played offstage. Seishin looks at the two with a happy expression. Sagobei, looking at Seishin's haggard form, weeps, wiping away the tears with a towel.

[33]

SAGOBEI (*weeping*): Ah! You have become so thin in the short time that you were away in prison. They have reason to call prison a hell on earth. The more I think about it the more pity I feel for you. It is my daughter who is wholly responsible for your present situation. I know very well that love is beyond our control, but the reason for your exile is Izayoi. This I cannot atone for. Please forgive me.

> *He presses his hands together in supplication.*

SEISHIN (*embarrassed*): Ah! When you tell me that, I am out of countenance before you. What blame is there on Izayoi? I suffered the humiliation of arrest only because I gave in to passions forbidden to a priest. I have nobody to blame. This was all due to the inclinations of this stupid priest. Truly, this is the punishment of the Buddha. On no account must you trouble your heart about it.

SAGOBEI: But to become like this—a shadow of your former self....

SEISHIN: Ah, don't bring up the past. Nothing will undo that now.

> *He pats Kyōgetsu on the head.*

SEISHIN (*touched*): I am glad you came to see me.

KYŌGETSU: I learned today that you were going to be exiled to a distant place. I was not sure whether I would ever see you again. As this may be the last time, I came to thank you for having taught me the sutras.

SEISHIN: That was very commendable of you. I am grateful that you came to see me. You were under my tutelage barely a year. There are those whom I taught longer. But how fickle people are. When one falls

[34]

on evil days no one comes near you. Only you have come. I am very happy.

SAGOBEI: Oh, Kyōgetsu is wiser than his years. Since yesterday he has been after me with, "Sagobei, if you are going, take me with you." From early this morning he kept saying, "Come, let us go! Aren't you ready yet?" He dragged me after him.

> *Kyōgetsu then takes the paper-wrapped offerings from under his collar.*

KYŌGETSU: This is not much, but I saved it from the offerings given to me at funerals and memorial services. I would like to give it to you for spending money. Please use it.

> *He holds the packet out. Seishin is touched.*

SEISHIN: My heart is full of gratitude. You are barely eleven years old. Yet you would give me those offerings because in your tender heart you thought I would have a difficult time of it in exile. I am grateful to you.

> *He reverently lifts the packet to his forehead.*

SEISHIN: I will accept your word for the deed. There are a number of senior disciples who are now heads of temples. If I seek them out along the way and travel on their charity, I will not need your offerings. Take them home with you.

KYŌGETSU: No, no. I saved them expressly for you. Please take them.

SEISHIN: Your words are sufficient. Take these home with you and buy yourself the books you like or something else.

KYŌGETSU: No, no. You cannot make me take them back.

SEISHIN: But I am unworthy of these offerings.

> *The two push the offerings back and forth. Sagobei breaks in.*

SAGOBEI: Oh, come, come, Seishin. He does this out of concern for your welfare. Why don't you condescend to accept his kindness? After all, no matter how much you insist, he will not take them back.

SEISHIN: Then I will accept your kindness.

KYŌGETSU (*pleased*) You will?

SEISHIN: With gratitude.

KYŌGETSU: Ah, thank you!

> *Seishin slips the packet under his collar.*

SEISHIN: Sagobei, look at Kyōgetsu. He is mature for one so young. The boy makes me think of my own youth. I was born the son of a fisherman in the outskirts of Funabashi in Shimōfusa. My only brother was kidnaped when he was ten and we never found him. Worried sick over him, both my parents died miserably. I was without anyone to look after me. To pray for the repose of their souls I became a disciple at Paradise Temple. My master there used to say I would make a fine priest. Look at me now. Kyōgetsu, you were born with a fine mind. When you grow up, devote yourself wholeheartedly to the way of the Buddha, and do not stray into evil ways. Don't compound evil deeds by thinking that the first time no one will know, and the second time will not matter. They will not be overlooked by the Buddha or the bodhisattvas. Sentence from above awaits you in the end. You will heap disgrace upon the teacher to whom you owe a debt of obligation, and your punishment will be exile. All the diligent training will come to

[36]

nothing in a twinkling. One error will undo the careful work of years. I am a good example of that. Persevere and let nothing deflect you from your aim. You will end up with your own temple.

KYŌGETSU (*solemnly*): I am obliged to you for your advice. I swear that I will do my best.

SAGOBEI: Remember what Seishin told you when you grow up. Be a good priest. Oh! What with the business with Kyōgetsu here, I had forgotten. Here is the wadded silk gown my daughter sent over yesterday with instructions that it be given to you. Throw away your dirty clothes and dress in something clean.

> *He takes out the silk gown from its cloth wrapper.*

SEISHIN: (*astonished*): You mean Izayoi made this garment and is giving it to me?

SAGOBEI: Yes. A gown, an undergarment, a sash, a towel, and even a pair of slippers.

SEISHIN (*moved*): Ah! What a touching kindness for someone in the pleasure quarters! I accept them gratefully.

SAGOBEI: Come, exchange your dirty clothes for clean ones as quickly as you can.

SEISHIN: No. To wear them as I am would soil them. I will put these on after I clean myself at the baths.

SAGOBEI: To be sure. That is a good idea. Where do you intend to go from there?

SEISHIN: As I am embarrassed to be seen, I will quit this place tonight. I will stay in Kyoto for a while to train myself anew to become a true priest. Izayoi may think me untrue to our vows, but tell her that under the present circumstances, our affair is ended and she must resign herself to that fact.

[37]

SAGOBEI: Ah! That is a commendable resolution! The truth is that I did not approve of a person in your position doing what you did. But even though I felt that it was a bad business, I could do nothing about it after you became lovers. But wisdom comes with experience, they say. You showed good sense when you said that you will take this opportunity to renounce her completely. Of course, when my daughter hears that you have gone to Kyoto forever, I fully expect her to protest. But as her father, I will make her give you up, no matter what she says, since it will be for your sake, whom she loves and cherishes. Please have no concern.

SEISHIN (*with a touch of regret*): The fact is that I would like to see her once more without her seeing me. But I am afraid that if I did, I would be reluctant to part from her.

SAGOBEI: It would be better not to see her. But when I say this, Seishin, please do not think that I looked the other away and let you see my daughter while you were at the Paradise Temple but that I ask you not to now because of your disgrace. I swear by the Nyorai Buddha that such is not my intention.

SEISHIN: I know your heart. Why should I doubt you?

A temple bell tolls the hour.

SEISHIN: It should not be long before dusk. No matter how long we talk, the sorrows of parting will never end. Please leave me.

SAGOBEI (*sadly*): I take my leave of you, but somehow I feel we will never meet again. . . .

KYŌGETSU: . . . and I grieve at this parting.

SEISHIN: You are right. This is not a case where I can return in a year or two. . . .

SAGOBEI: ...and in interim of the long months and days
....

KYŌGETSU: ...in a world that is full of uncertainties....

SEISHIN: ...this may be our parting.

> *Seishin takes Kyōgetsu's hands.*

SAGOBEI: Ah, do not say such an unpropitious thing! The gods protect us!

SEISHIN: Then if fortune smiles on us....

SAGOBEI: ...we will, in time....

SEISHIN and SAGOBEI: ...see each other again.

> *Sagobei and Kyōgetsu rise.*

KYŌGETSU: Goodbye, Seishin.

SEISHIN: Learn your sutras well.

KYŌGETSU: I will.

SAGOBEI: Come, let us go.

> *To a song offstage and a bell tolling, Sagobei and Kyōgetsu exit hand in hand down the runway. Seishin watches them go.*

SEISHIN: How thoughtful that wise little Kyōgetsu is, even of me. He shows every sign of becoming a fine priest in the future. But the precept against carnal desire is difficult to observe. Ah! I hope he will be spared my fate. It is already dusk. This suits me fine. I will leave as quickly as I can before people see me.

> *He rises, carrying the bundle.*

SEISHIN (*wavering*): But wait. I have renounced her, but Izayoi and I were inseparable these last two years. If I could have just one more glimpse of her....

[39]

> *With his hand, he gestures as though to banish such a thought.*

SEISHIN: Ah! Passion, like a dog, will not leave me though I drive it away. I prostrate myself before the Amida Buddha! Hail to the Amida Buddha!

> *He prays reverently. The stage set revolves to the sound of temple bells.*

II. 2

Time: evening of the same day

> *The scene: the Hundred Piles Breakwater. Along the full length of the stage, a raised level, two feet high, represents a stone wall. At stage left is the breakwater piling. Also at stage left a Buddhist altar with its rear to the audience is set on the raised level. At stage right a pine branch overhangs a bamboo fence. The entire down stage area represents water.*
> *The bell tolls and there is drum and flute music until the set comes to rest.*
> *Suddenly there is a commotion, and Kane, an unlicensed prostitute, runs out from the crossroads shrine pursued by Ichisuke, the footman from the previous scene.*

ICHISUKE (*furiously*): Hey, hey, you slut! Give me back those hundred coppers!

KANE: Give them back my eye! You didn't pay me for last night.

ICHISUKE (*indignantly*): That was on the cuff last night. Even so a hundred coppers are too much when it should only be twenty-four. I need a little money tonight, so give me the change.

KANE: (*soothingly*): Don't be such a tightwad. I will show you a good time.

ICHISUKE (*curtly*): Not tonight. I told you I need the money. I can't be hanging about.

KANE (*equally curt*): If you don't have the time tonight, come tomorrow night.

>   *She prepares to go. Ichisuke grabs her.*

ICHISUKE (*threateningly*): So you won't return it even after I have pleaded with you?

KANE (*scoffingly*): Why should I?

ICHISUKE (*seeing red*): You slut! I'll teach you a lesson or two!

>   *He seizes the edge of Kane's sash. Kane resorts to masculine gestures for comic effect.*

KANE: What impudence!

>   *The two scuffle in knockabout fashion, fighting for possession of the coppers. They drop the bag. They cannot locate it in the dark.*

KANE (*dismayed*): Oh, oh! What a calamity! I dropped the money!

ICHISUKE: What? You dropped it?

KANE: Find it and I will give you half.

>   *They search. He finds the money and a rolled poster.*

ICHISUKE: I found the money and this thing.

KANE: Read it quickly and see if we can turn it into cash.

ICHISUKE: I hope I can read it without stumbling.

He unrolls the poster

ICHISUKE: "The title of the following musical narrative is 'The Early Evening Moon Seen Through the Plum and Willow Trees'. The singer is Kiyomoto Enjudayū and the samisen player is Kiyomoto Tokubei. The actors are Iwai Kumesaburō and Ichikawa Kodanji."

KANE (*disappointed*): Oh, bosh! That's only a poster for the musical narrative in this scene.

ICHISUKE (*businesslike*): Come on, you promised. Hand over half.

KANE: Not on your life!

ICHISUKE (*furiously*): You whore! I'll take it away from you if that's the last thing I do!

KANE: Oh, stop harping on the same old tune!

ICHISUKE (*suddenly stepping out of character*): Oh, that reminds me, I must make the announcement: Ladies and gentlemen! The musical narrative for which you have been waiting now begins!

KANE: We are the ones who called the tune!

ICHISUKE: Get away with you!

> *Then to the rapid drumbeats which are a convention in the kabuki in scenes laid near water, plus flute music, Kane exits running to stage left with Ichisuke in pursuit. A section of the paling at stage right then falls open, revealing the Kiyomoto musicians on a platform. The music begins.*

NARRATOR: Even on a hazy moonlit night the images of the stars number one, two, three, four, five. "Five

strokes on the alarm bell? Am I being pursued?"
Fleeing the quarter, Izayoi hears the tolling of the hour
bell with a beating heart.

> *To samisen music and the ringing of a*
> *bell, Izayoi comes swiftly up the runway.*
> *She is dressed in the casual dress of a*
> *prostitute, with a sash of soft silk. A*
> *kerchief is draped over the head. She stops*
> *on the runway.*

NARRATOR: Izayoi comes, fleeing along the frosty river's
edge with an anxious heart. She is pursued by the wind,
and flies she knows not where. She dreads the eyes of
men more than the whitefish does the bonfire and the
nets of a fisherman's boat.

> *Izayoi pantomimes on the runway, then*
> *comes to the stage proper.*

IZAYOI: Oh, what a relief to know that the voices I heard
were not those of my pursuers! I knew that Seishin was
being exiled today. My father and I are obligated to
him. I longed to see him and escaped from the brothel.
I have come this far but I have lost my way in the dark.
I pray that I might be able to see him!

NARRATOR: She stops for a moment. Upstream, from a
pleasure boat returning from a plum-viewing party,
comes a song: "If you want to meet your lover in
secret, avoid a pitch-black night. Your luck on the
sixteenth night, the *izayoi,* when no clouds conceal the
moon, will be good. Wait patiently until then." Taking
this as a lucky omen, Izayoi prepares to hurry on.

> *Izayoi starts to exit at stage left. Then*
> *Seishin enters at stage left, dressed in a*
> *plain, elegant gown. He wears a black*
> *hood. They pass, avoiding each others*

[43]

> *eyes. The moon appears, and their eyes meet.*

SEISHIN (*astonished*): Aren't you Izayoi?

IZAYOI: You are Seishin?

SEISHIN (*with mixed feelings of joy and distress*): Ah, an unfortunate meeting!

> *He starts to go, but Izayoi catches hold of him.*

IZAYOI (*with feeling*): How I have longed to see you!

NARRATOR: From the openings of her sleeves comes the fragrance of plum blossoms as she clings to him. He is soon charmed.

> *Izayoi detains Seishin. Seishin realizes that there is no way out of this situation now.*

SEISHIN (*suppressing his feelings*): You're all alone. Where are you going in the dark and so far from the quarter?

IZAYOI (*crushed*): Where? Oh, Seishin, how heartless of you! Yesterday my father told me that you were to be expelled and that I would never again see you in the quarter. When I heard him say that he thought you might be starting on a journey somewhere, I just had to see you. At the quarter every omen was evil and pointed to a long separation. I decided to leave and sneaked out at sundown. I did this because I wanted to see you.

SEISHIN (*softening*): I thought I could never see you again. But it was foreordained that I would run across you here. What have I done in my previous existence to deserve your kindness? Look at what I am now. Only today I received these clothes from you. It is thanks to you that I will be able to go to my friends with my head high.

[44]

IZAYOI: You speak of friends. Where are you going from here?

SEISHIN: I am not sure where I am going. But having been exiled, I cannot remain here. When I leave this place, I think I will seek out an acquaintance in Kyoto and get his help.

IZAYOI (*pleadingly*): In that case, please take me along with you.

SEISHIN: (*troubled*): Having sworn my love to you until the next world, I want to take you along with me. But Izayoi, listen to the reasons I cannot: by some delusion of the heart I broke my vow of chastity and have been banished. I have disgraced not only myself but have heaped shame upon the name of my teacher to whom I am forever indebted.

NARRATOR: Seishin will take everything up to now for a dream and revert to his original aim.

SEISHIN (*with determination*): I will give you up, go to Kyoto, and renew my aim of attaining the way of a priest. You must return to the quarter. I understand your term of indenture is long. Choose a good client and entrust yourself to him. Remember that your first duty is to your father.

IZAYOI: You are cruel, Seishin.

NARRATOR (*The entreaty*): "You might think that I am reproaching you when I tell you this, but I did not become infatuated with a priest out of wantonness or as a passing fancy, nor was I fickle. I swear on the Amida Buddha that I would gladly wear a nun's habits into the next world. But you must be a demon in the guise of a priest to tell me after our long separation to sever our ties. I will not hear of it," she says, and clings to him. Her bitterness and grief are not feigned.

[45]

> *Izayoi pantomimes to the lyrics and weeps,*
> *clinging to Seishin.*

SEISHIN: I am moved that your love for me is so deep. But stop and think how ill-matched we are. Even in outward appearance I am not an ordinary man but an unfrocked priest. You, on the other hand, are celebrated in Ōiso. How can I consent to your coming with me? Everyone will laugh at you. People will say, "Aren't there other men in the world? What peculiar tastes that Izayoi has!" You know the saying that a mismatch leads to trouble.

IZAYOI (*earnestly*): The other prostitutes may act fickle to make their hard life in the quarter bearable. But for me there is only one man to whom I would give myself for life. You have been considerate not only of me but of my father as well. You were so kind that I even thought that if you should die, I would die with you. But what harsh words just now! You will not change your mind?

SEISHIN (*gruffly*): Come, it is for your own good. Go back to the quarter as quickly as you can and serve out your term.

IZAYOI (*as though to herself*): Those words will echo in my ears in Hades.

NARRATOR: The branches of the willow tree that leans over the bank droop into the water.

> *Izayoi, looking reproachfully at Seishin,*
> *resolves to die.*

IZAYOI (*with eyes closed, invokes the Buddha*): All hail to the Amida Buddha!

NARRATOR: Izayoi has decided to die. Seishin frantically seizes her.

> *Izayoi moves to throw herself into the*

[46]

> *river downstage. Seishin throws his arms*
> *around her.*

SEISHIN: Ah, wait! Don't be rash!

IZAYOI (*in despair*): Let me go! Let me die!

SEISHIN (*wretchedly*): This is madness! If I let you die, your father and brother will bear a grudge against me. It would be murder added to my other sin. How can I be a party to your death?

IZAYOI: But when I think of the consequences, I have all the more reason for dying.

SEISHIN: What's this? What is the reason?

IZAYOI: I am embarrassed to tell you. After all I am a prostitute. But I am with your....

SEISHIN: What? My child?

IZAYOI: Yes. For two months.

> *She pantomimes shame.*

SEISHIN: Oh!

> *He expresses stunned surprise. To under-*
> *line the pathos of the scene, samisen and*
> *flute music is played.*

IZAYOI: Now you know why I cannot return to the quarter and why I have decided to drown myself. If you have pity for me, please say a mass for me.

> *Seishin realizes there is no way to ex-*
> *tricate himself from this situation.*

SEISHIN (*in despair*): If you should die now, I would be condemning not only you but the child in your womb to a fate without salvation. But if I were to take you along....

NARRATOR: ...I would be an abductor if I am caught,

[47]

because you have escaped from the quarter....

SEISHIN: ···and I would again be arrested. I feel everything closing in around me. I do not have the heart to let you die, and yet I cannot take you along with me. This is a hopeless situation. I will....

IZAYOI: Will you die with me?

SEISHIN (*resigned*): There is no other way.

NARRATOR: "What an ill-fated coincidence that Izayoi is three years older than her name and is in her unlucky nineteenth year, while I am also in my unlucky twenty-fifth. To part now is to turn our backs on the joys of life, just as the wild geese wing home without waiting for the cherry blossoms to bloom. They fly to the distant lands of the north. We go to the Pure Land of the West trusting in the vow of the Amida to save all men. All hail, all hail, all hail to the Amida Buddha. Is this our parting in this world?" they say and embrace. The moon is misty with signs of rain.

> *The two resolve to die and pantomime regret at parting. They take each other's hands and, their eyes locked, draw together. The music ends, and a temple bell tolls the hour.*

SEISHIN (*in despair*): An evil karma prevents our union in this world.

IZAYOI: We have made up our minds to die.

SEISHIN: Before we run into the searchers from the quarter....

IZAYOI: ...let us leap hand in hand into the river....

SEISHIN: ...in a love suicide that will be a scandal....

IZAYOI: ...for tomorrow we will be the gossip of the world.

SEISHIN: When he hears that gossip....

IZAYOI: ...how grieved father will be.

SEISHIN: Think of that, too, as having been foreordained.

IZAYOI: ...father, and our unfilial act of dying before you....

SEISHIN: ...will you forgive?

SEISHIN and IZAYOI: Hail to the Amida Buddha!

NARRATOR: They look toward the west, and the hands they press in supplication freeze. They leap into the icy river and a notoriety as lovers separated not even by death seems to be theirs.

> *The two lovers leap into the river. There is a loud splash and spray dashes up. The set revolves to samisen music and a beating drum suggests waves.*

II. 3

Time: Immediately following preceding scene.

> *At the rear of stage center is a sluice gate. On each side are high embankments and pine trees. The stage represents the river. At stage center is a netting boat with a burning torch to attract fish. A dipping net has been cast. In the boat are Haku-ren, a haiku poet who is in reality Ōdera Shōbei, the thief. He wears a hood of black crepe and a striped coat. Sanji, the boatman, has driven a pole into the river-bed and is mooring the boat to it. A merry boatman's ditty, and the sound of waves on the drum are played until the set comes to rest.*

[49]

SANJI (*cheerfully*): I say, Master, it looked for a while like a regular downpour, but luckily it's cleared up.

HAKUREN: We can't be too sure. The clouds are moving quite fast. There may be another shower. Let's quit with this one catch. The more we catch the harder it is to stop.

SANJI: If we haul in a good catch in two or three casts, let's call it a night. It's already close to ten o'clock.

HAKUREN (*surprised*): Close to ten? The nights really have become short. Well, then, it isn't a fancy place, but let's have something to eat at Funaji's before it closes.

SANJI: I'd like that. I know you don't drink, Master, but ah! there's nothing like swigging the wine you pour over a helping of double-size broiled eels. I'm ready for some right now.

HAKUREN: But eels are too oily, and bad for a tippler.

SANJI (*with conviction*): Not at all. Those who choose to eat sea slugs and fish fillets shriveled in cold water are giving themselves airs. To make a long story short, when it comes to food or women, they are not tasty when they are simple. Nothing is tasty unless it is rich and heavy and comes out on a belch.

HAKUREN (*laughing*): Then your regular girl at the Kotsu-kahara brothel must be to your liking, eh?

SANJI (*abashed*): You guessed it. I would like you to meet her one of these days. Her face is a sorry thing, like a balloon fish come in on the tide and stepped on. But even so, there is something about her.

HAKUREN (*laughing*): Here, here. I think you owe me something for listening to you carry on about your tender passion.

SANJI: I'll treat you to eels at Funaji's when we get there.

HAKUREN: That's fine.

SANJI: Not to change the subject, Master, but you often go to the pleasure quarters, too. That Izayoi at the Ōgiya—is she amusing? She seems very prim when she is at a party.

HAKUREN: You are right. She is entertaining, but I can stand a shade more amiability.

SANJI: Well, then, she's not a bit to your taste, is she? Well, I think it is time to draw up the net.

HAKUREN: Oh, I had completely forgotten about it.

He rises and tugs at the net.

HAKUREN: Something is caught in this. It's so heavy I can't pull it in.

SANJI: It may be garbage. Step aside, Master.

He tugs at the net.

SANJI (*puzzled*): You are right. This is confoundedly heavy.

He pulls with all his strength, and Izayoi is discovered enmeshed in the net.

SANJI: Hey! Something *is* caught in it.

HAKUREN: Yes. It's a woman.

SANJI (*alarmed*): Not a corpse!

HAKUREN: No, she must have jumped in just now. Help me pull her up.

SANJI (*dismayed*): What a thing to catch!

They lift Izayoi into the boat and attend to her.

SANJI: It's just as you said: she has only now jumped in.

HAKUREN: Yes, by the color in her face, the....

He looks closely at Izayoi.

[51]

HAKUREN (*incredulously*): Oh! This is Izayoi of the Ōgiya!

SANJI: What? Izayoi? You are right. It is.

> *Hakuren takes a stimulant from his wallet and puts it in Izayoi's mouth. Sanji fills a dipper with river water and brings it to Izayoi's lips. Hakuren holds her and rubs her chest.*

HAKUREN: Listen, Izayoi! Can you hear me?

SANJI: Izayoi! Izayoi!

> *Izayoi moans and revives.*

SANJI (*triumphantly*): We did it! We did it! She's breathing again!

HAKUREN: Are you all right? Pull yourself together.

IZAYOI (*coming to*): Yes, I know where I am. But I must die. Please let me die.

HAKUREN (*puzzled*): Why must you die, Izayoi?

> *Izayoi becomes aware of the speaker, looks at Hakuren, and is astonished.*

IZAYOI: Oh! Hakuren! Did you save me?

HAKUREN (*gravely*): What your reasons were I do not know. But your rescue by me is an act of the gods. You are not fated to die yet. To forsake this world seems a poor idea. Tell me, why must you die?

IZAYOI: Don't ask me that.

HAKUREN: I have done many a good deed in my time. Even if a total stranger had been in your place I would take every step to save him. I have known you. Why shouldn't I save you? As to why you must die, tell me the reasons. I am a man. Depending on the circumstances, you may count on me to solve your difficulties.

SANJI (*sympathetically*): Hear that, Izayoi? You can trust Master. Feel free to tell us the reasons.

IZAYOI: Well, I cannot....

HAKUREN: It never hurts to talk things over. Tell me about it.

Samisen music begins.

IZAYOI (*feigning*): To tell you this when things have come to this pass is embarrassing. But I had been ill for some time and had been absent from the establishment. Then the three of them—my secret lover, the lady of the house, and the matron—beat me. They said I was pretending to be sick. Even a lowly prostitute falls ill, and when she does how can she receive customers? When I didn't show myself the matron flogged me cruelly. I was desperate and rather than be tortured to death, I chose drowning. I escaped from the quarter determined to die here.

HAKUREN: That was foolish of you. You showed poor judgment. Death is no solution.

IZAYOI: It's easy for you to say that. You don't know what it is to be a prostitute.

HAKUREN: What if I offered your owner a lump sum and bought you out?

IZAYOI (*in disbelief*): What?

HAKUREN: As I just told you, it was by the command of the gods that I rescued you. When I buy you out, I ask you to put yourself completely in my hands for three days. Then, if you have a lover, I will agree to becoming your brother and standing in as a relative to marry you to him. I understand you have a father. Don't you have any feeling of obligation to him? It is unfilial to think that you are free to destroy yourself. Who do you think brought you up? Think again about dying.

[53]

IZAYOI (*moved*): How can I thank you for your kindness? I am moved to tears. But if I live....

SANJI (*urgently*): Come, come, Izayoi. What is there to think about? You heard what Master just said. He's prepared to unite you with your lover if you have one. That's what the magnanimous Yuranosuke says to the prostitute Okaru in the play. If you insist on dying, there must be another reason.

IZAYOI: No, no, there is no other reason.

SANJI: If not, why not consent?

IZAYOI: Even you take his side. I am grateful. Then, until I deliver my....

HAKUREN (*puzzled*): What?

IZAYOI (*quickly recovering*): I mean, when I am delivered from bondage, how happy my father will be.

HAKUREN (*with relief*): Now that you've changed your mind, let's not waste a moment. I will send Sanji to the quarter tonight to settle the matter.

IZAYOI: But such a large sum of money.

HAKUREN: Don't worry. It's not much. But here, you're soaking wet. You'll get chilled on the way to my place. Let's borrow some clothes from Ogin in Yanagibashi.

SANJI: Oh, you mean Ogin, the head geisha at the Waka-take house? Her clothes will fit Izayoi exactly.

HAKUREN: Well, let's get the boat to the bank.

SANJI: All right.

> *Sanji unties the rope. Faint wave effects on the drum. Izayoi looks upstream.*

IZAYOI (*mournfully*): You must be....

HAKUREN: What did you say?

[54]

IZAYOI: You must be married.

HAKUREN (*gruffly*): What if I am? I'll set you up in a separate house.

IZAYOI: And when your wife finds out?

HAKUREN: How timid you are.

SANJI: Look out, we're off!

> *He poles and the boat moves off.*

IZAYOI: Oh!

> *She staggers and falls toward Hakuren, who catches her.*

HAKUREN: This is not bad at all!

> *Sanji leers at them.*

SANJI (*shouting*): We're heading for port!

> *The stage revolves to the sound of waves and a gay tune.*

II. 4

Time: Simultaneously with preceding scene

> *Scene: the Hundred Piles Breakwater. Narrative chanting in the Takemoto style begins.*

NARRATOR: Moving across the sky the rain clouds pour pale gray ink. Legend has it that a temple bell sank at this spot in the river long ago. But because he learned to swim, Seishin cannot sink, try as he might.

> *Seishin surfaces and holds onto a pile. He climbs up onto the raised level.*

SEISHIN: I am buoyed up by the water and cannot drown. Brought up as I was in the fishing village of Gyōtoku in Shimōsa, learning to swim was no trick. This skill is now a hindrance to my following Izayoi. How wretched I am!

NARRATOR: Seishin gazes at the river with a look of self-reproach.

SEISHIN: But Izayoi has drowned. Formless as it was, my seed in her womb....

NARRATOR: ...has gone—ah, woe!—journeying with her to the Land of the Shades. I will follow them and we will cross the river Sanzu in the land of the dead. A dead infant piles pebbles on the banks of the river Sai until he is saved by the bodhisattva Jizō. And it is stones that Seishin now puts in his sleeve pockets for ballast. What a contrast to his heavy heart is the gay music from upstream. It comes from a pleasure boat returning from a plum-viewing.

> *Seishin picks up some stones and slips them into his sleeves to provide weight. Then a boat appears at stage left and sounds of revelry are heard.*

SEISHIN (*disturbed*): Oh, for tranquillity to meditate on the Buddha! I wish to be led straight to paradise. But that music makes my mind stray.

NARRATOR: He presses his hands together in supplication. A soft spring rain falls like mist. How is Motome, the young page, to know that a sad fate awaits him here? With drops of rain that will soon turn into tears falling from his umbrella, Motome comes.

> *Seishin leans against a pile and gazes at the boat. Motome comes up the runway wearing a long-sleeved gown, a sword, and wooden clogs. He carries an umbrella. He speaks on the runway.*

MOTOME (*anxiously*): That must have been the midnight

[56]

bell. I had intended to return earlier, but a sudden rain came on, and I wasted more time than I should looking for an umbrella.

> *Seishin is distracted by the music. He and Motome soliloquize.*

SEISHIN (*in desperation*): Ah! How little of other people's suffering do they know. They weaken my resolve.

MOTOME: My father told me yesterday that he had to have some money by today.

SEISHIN: The ups and downs of men's fortunes, to be rich or poor, were foreordained. Why should one bother to struggle?

MOTOME: I had to ask Lord Mondo of the Ōe family to lend me the money.

SEISHIN: It is one way to live riotously and gaily in the company of geisha and male entertainers.

MOTOME: Oh, to get this to father as quickly as possible. He will be overjoyed!

SEISHIN: To stand begging at a gate in rags and on the verge of starvation: that, too, is a way of life.

MOTOME (*in distress*): In my anxiety to make haste I feel a chronic pain coming on.

SEISHIN: To drown: this, too, is one's man's life.

MOTOME: Is there no tree to rest under, to ease the pain in my stomach?

SEISHIN: My impure mind prevents me from killing myself.

MOTOME (*in desperation*): Oh, why can't I go faster?

SEISHIN: What am I....

SEISHIN and MOTOME: ...to do?

[57]

NARRATOR: In each heart there are troubled thoughts that are like torn clouds. Their gloomy thoughts become darker. There is another downpour. Motome doubles up with painful spasms.

> *Seishin leans against a pile and listens intently to the sounds of merry-making coming from the boat. Motome, in agony, comes to the main stage staggering and pressing his chest.*

MOTOME: Sir! Sir!

> *He claps Seishin on the back. Seishin is startled.*

SEISHIN: Who's that?

MOTOME: It is I.

SEISHIN: Who are you?

MOTOME: A passerby.

SEISHIN (*relieved*): You're only a young boy. What has happened?

MOTOME (*gasping*): I can hardly take a step with this pain. If you have some medicine would you be good enough to give me some?

SEISHIN: You took me so completely by surprise I thought you were a ghost. But you must be in terrible pain. If I had any medicine on me I would give it to you, but I have only just pulled myself.... Oh, I mean the nearest doctor is about two hundred yards across the river. This is a problem!

MOTOME: Oh, it's painful!

SEISHIN: Here, let me rub your chest to ease the spasms.

MOTOME: Thank you.

SEISHIN: Now, then, where does it hurt?

NARRATOR: The fingers that slip under the collar of the suffering Motome contact a purse.

> *Motome suffers agonies. Seishin props him up and puts his hand under the foldover collar. He feels a purse there.*

SEISHIN: What is this, young man?

MOTOME: That's my money.

SEISHIN: It seems like quite a large sum.

MOTOME: Yes. I have fifty gold pieces.

SEISHIN (*astonished*): What?

NARRATOR: At this, Seishin involuntarily releases the pressure. With a groan Motome falls back.

> *Seishin is so surprised at the sum mentioned that his hand relaxes. Motome falls.*

SEISHIN: Ah! Don't bend backward! Hold on!

NARRATOR: Taking a towel, he dips it into the river for water to bring to the fainting boy.

> *Seishin tends to Motome.*

SEISHIN: Young man! Young man! Don't let yourself go!

NARRATOR: He calls him back to life.

> *Motome revives.*

MOTOME: I feel much better.

SEISHIN: Has the pain subsided?

MOTOME: Yes, thanks to your care.

SEISHIN: And where are you going in the dead of night with such a large sum on you?

MOTOME: Well, this precious sum is for someone my father owes an obligation to. The person is in distress. We need it by tonight, which is why I am out so late.

[59]

Now by bad luck an attack of cramps has delayed me.
How anxiously my father must be waiting for me!

SEISHIN: So that's it! But it is dangerous to be on the road
at night with money. Take a palanquin. About two
hundred yards from here there is a public palanquin
stand at the crossroads.

MOTOME: Thank you, I will.

NARRATOR: Motome bows and rises.

SEISHIN: By some strange fate, we were meant to exchange
words under this willow tree on the banks of this river.

MOTOME: It was part of the unending chain of fate that
we are linked to the current of the Inase River.

SEISHIN: However much we were fated to meet, we must,
like the ice that freezes in the night and in the morning
breaks. . . .

MOTOME: . . . part, each to go his separate way like the
waves.

SEISHIN: Whoever you may be, and wherever you are
from. . . .

MOTOME: . . . if fate should will it. . . .
SEISHIN: . . . we will meet again.

MOTOME: Farewell.

He starts to go.

SEISHIN (*impulsively*): Wait.

He plucks at Motome's sleeve.

MOTOME: What is it?

SEISHIN: Be careful.

NARRATOR: Reluctantly, Seishin lets go of Motome's
sleeve. Both are fated by the law that says "even the
merest brushing of the sleeves of strangers is ordained

[60]

is another life." They part, and Motome goes. Seishin gazes after him, and an evil thought takes shape in his breast.

> *Motome exits at stage right. Alone, Seishin is lost in thought; then he exits at stage right in pursuit of Motome. There is a commotion and Motome enters running, with Seishin after him.*

NARRATOR: It is no trouble at all for Seishin to overtake Motome and remove the purse. Motome seizes his hand.

MOTOME (*panic-stricken*): You can't mean to take this money!

SEISHIN (*desperately*): You are shocked. But it was fate that I should have discovered the money when I helped you ease the pain. I know this is evil. I have reproved myself. But the thought persisted and I must use force. I know I am asking the unreasonable but resign yourself to having been trapped by a villain, and lend me the money.

MOTOME (*aghast*): What? Then your kindness and sympathy were all a deception to steal this from me?

SEISHIN: Not at first. I was sincere when I nursed you. There you were, a young lad suffering in the rain. But it was just your misfortune to have money on you. If you did not, I would not have fallen prey to temptation. Those high-living people in the boat make me envious of their way of life. You will no doubt think me a demon, a priest going against the true path, wicked and inhuman. But let me fall into the bottomless hell for condemned priests. I want to live to the full and taste the joys of the Pure Land in this world. It's no good your appealing to reason. I must have the money.

MOTOME (*fiercely*): And you expect me to hand it to you?

[61]

NARRATOR: Drawing his sword he slashes without warning. Seishin skillfully takes the blow with Motome's umbrella. As they parry and dodge, the sounds of revelry are heard again.

> *Motome unsheathes a short sword and swings at Seishin who parries with the umbrella. At the end of the narrator's line, a gay song is heard in the boat. Seishin runs toward stage left. Motome cuts off a pile at a sharp angle. Seishin strikes down Motome's sword and knocks the wind out of him. Motome staggers downstage, collapses over the pile with the knife edge, and cuts his throat.*

MOTOME: Murder! Murder!

SEISHIN: It's now or never.

NARRATOR: There is no response. Seishin is unaware that the boy is dying and snatches at the purse that had brought the two together in a fateful encounter. The drawstring catches around Motome's neck and sends him into the throes of death. Sad is the end of one so young. He is like a bud that falls.

SEISHIN: Here, lad! Speak! What? Dead? Oh!

> *He is aghast. Samisen and flute music.*

SEISHIN (*in anguish*): This money no longer serves the purpose for which I wanted it. Izayoi's father could have used it for her funeral, but how will money gained by murder give her soul any rest?

> *He casts the money aside. He sees Motome's sword.*

SEISHIN: There's the answer! Izayoi still guides me from her grave. Die by the sword, she says, if not by drown-

[62]

ing. Look, lad, I will die by your sword in atonement. Then to the land of the dead with you and Izayoi. That is my penance. Yes, that's the way!

> *Seishin prepares to rip open his belly. A full moon emerges from behind a cloud. Now Seishin shows his true colors.*

SEISHIN: But wait a moment. Who knows that Izayoi has drowned? Or that I killed this boy for his money? Only the moon and I. A man lives only fifty years. If all goes well, he prospers ten or twenty years at most. Money opens doors even for a man in rags. If it's all the same, you might as well live as though there were no tomorrow—like those people. Whether I take the life of one man or a thousand, I have only one life to give. I've made the plunge into crime. Now what shall I be? A thief, a housebreaker. I will live in luxury on what belongs to others. Whatever possessed me to think that I wanted to die?

NARRATOR: Seishin suffers a swift change of heart. This is the birth of Seikichi the Demon Thief about whom men tell tales.

> *Seishin throws the sword into the river and picks up Motome.*

SEISHIN: Now for a water burial.

> *He throws Motome into the river. Rain falls.*

SEISHIN: Ah! Rain again.

> *A temple bell tolls. Hakuren and Izayoi enter at stage left under an umbrella. He carries a lantern. They bump into Seishin. Hakuren puts out the lantern. Rapid plucking on one note on the samisen—a*

> *convention in scenes of suspense.*
> *Startled, Seishin drops the purse.*

HAKUREN: What was that?

SEISHIN: Ah!

> *In stylized, choreographed movements,*
> *they grope about for the money. Sanji the*
> *boatman comes in between Seishin and*
> *Hakuren. He stumbles across the purse*
> *and picks it up.*

SANJI (*overjoyed*): This feels like a lot more than a hundred coppers!

> *Seishin snatches the bag away. Sanji*
> *grapples with him but Seishin knocks the*
> *wind out of him with a strong blow.*
> *Hakuren leads Izayoi by the hand and*
> *starts toward the runway. With the purse*
> *between his teeth, Seishin flips Sanji over.*
> *At the same moment Hakuren shifts the*
> *umbrella from one hand to the other. On*
> *this cue, the end-of-act clappers are*
> *struck offstage. Seishin raises the bag of*
> *money to his forehead and grins ferociously.*
> *Hakuren and Izayoi exit down the runway. To rapid beats on the clappers and*
> *drum, and to gay samisen music, the*
> *curtain is drawn.*

ACT FOUR SCENE ONE

Time: A month later.

The scene: the anteroom of Izayoi's house in Hase Lane. She is now Hakuren's concubine.

At stage center is the raised set of an apartment. Upstage is an entrance curtained off with printed cotton. Two samisen are hung on the walls. At stage left an apartment is fitted with paper sliding doors. Downstage at right is a gate. Stage right is the entrance into an alley. Mokusuke, the manservant, who is the magistrate Terasawa in disguise, is chopping some duck bones on a block of wood. Nearby, Sanji looks on smoking a pipe. The curtain is drawn to a song accompanied by samisen, drum, and flute.

SANJI: You're busy, aren't you, Mokusuke?

MOKUSUKE: These are for me, so it's no trouble at all. The Master and his mistress get the breasts and other parts. The bones and skin come down to Yone and me.

SANJI (*enviously*): You lucky dog! So you're going to pick at these with the good-looking Yone, eh? Hmmm. A cozy meal for two. That's a heap of bones for one bird, isn't it?

MOKUSUKE: Well, I left as much meat as I could, seeing as we were going to get them.

SANJI: I wouldn't mind having some myself.

> *Hempuku, a haiku poet, dressed for calling with a wooden sword; and Ginshichi, a second-hand furniture dealer, got up like a haiku poet, come up the runway toward the stage.*

GINSHICHI (*self-consciously*): Tell me, Master Hempuku, do I look like haiku poet in my get up?

HEMPUKU (*half-heartedly*): Don't you worry about that. I swear you do. Nobody would take you for anything else. There's no danger of your being unmasked.

GINSHICHI (*still worried*): I only hope no one will show me up for what I am—a second-hand furniture dealer.

HEMPUKU: Just leave everything to me.

GINSHICHI: Anyway, what interests me more is the fact that Hakuren is a rich man and has a pretty mistress.

HEMPUKU: He's a very understanding man. You won't lose anything by knowing him.

GINSHICHI: Well, then, let's be on our way.

> *They continue to the stage.*

HEMPUKU: Hello, is the master at home?

MOKUSUKE: Oh, it's you, Hempuku. Yes, he is. Come in.

HEMPUKU: We're in luck. Follow me, sir.

GINSHICHI: Thank you.

They enter the anteroom. Sanji sees them.

SANJI: Well, it's you, Hempuku.

HEMPUKU: Ah, Sanji! How is fishing these days?

SANJI: What with this south wind the fish have gone upstream quite a ways.

GINSHICHI (*trying to be witty*): When the whitefish begin to carry eggs they're no good, are they?

He says this in a high-pitched voice.

MOKUSUKE (*offended*): I say, Hempuku, who is that person with the peculiar voice?

HEMPUKU: This is a friend of mine, a well-known poet. I brought him along to introduce him to Hakuren.

GINSHICHI (*clumsily*): I want to make the acquaintance of the master and bask in the presence of the beautiful mistress.

HEMPUKU (*upset*): Here, don't carry on so.

GINSHICHI: Is the junk-dealer showing?

HEMPUKU (*covering*): Ahem! Oh, a duck dish, eh, Mokusuke? That's tasty, but give me sliced raw flounder any day. I even like it a day old.

GINSHICHI (*blundering on*): Right you are! When you eat it with horseradish, your nose stings and tears fall.

MOKUSUKE (*earnestly*): Talk about tears! Let me tell you about prices for ducks around here. They're so cheap where I come from. There are a lot of them quacking away in the pond in the back, but Shinkō the fisherman sold me this today for a small fortune.

SANJI: Don't blame him. He just took advantage of your simple-mindedness.

GINSHICHI: Innocence in a woman is charming, but in a man....

[67]

HEMPUKU: An excellent observation!

> *Izayoi's maid Yone enters. She is dressed in the garb of a servant girl, and carries a dish.*

YONE: Oh, sirs, you are welcome.

HEMPUKU: Ah, Yone, a happy New Year to you.

YONE: The same to you, sir.

MOKUSUKE: Well, Yone, do you want something?

YONE: Master said to bring the bones over when you've chopped them up.

MOKUSUKE: What? He wants these? But he never did before.

YONE: He doesn't usually, but he wants them tonight.

MOKUSUKE: He must have seen me leave all this meat on. Crime will out!

SANJI (*slyly*): Well, you got cheated, didn't you?

MOKUSUKE: Confound it!

HEMPUKU, GINSHICHI, SANJI: That is very kind of him.

YONE: Master told me to tell you to go inside. Hempuku, Ginshichi, Sanji: That is very kind of him.

SANJI: Well, let's feast on the bones Mokusuke took so much pains to chop up!

MOKUSUKE: Oh, do what you like!

GINSHICHI: I'm more interested in the doxy.

HEMPUKU: Stop prattling.

YONE: Please go in, gentlemen.

SANJI: Shall we?

HEMPUKU: After you.

> *They all go inside. Mokusuke is left alone.*

[68]

MOKUSUKE: I went to all that trouble for what I thought would be a good meal. But after they get through with it there won't be even a mouthful for me. All I can do now is lick the chopping board.

> *He looks resentfully at the block. At this point, Ofuji, Hakuren's wife, dressed in the costume of a townsman's wife, comes up the runway. She is attended by her maid Tora.*

OFUJI: I think you were right, Tora. My husband must be at Izayoi's place.

TORA (*with hostility*): Really, what a horrid master to leave you guarding the nest alone night after night! Why don't you break into their bedroom and have it out with her. It's because you are so good-hearted that this has happened.

OFUJI: I'm going to speak my mind tonight. That's why I've asked you to come to back me up.

TORA (*confidently*): I can trounce any woman I care to. Come, let's hurry.

> *They come to the stage. Tora opens the gate.*

TORA: Mokusuke! Mokusuke!

MOKUSUKE: Coming, coming. Who is it? Why, it's Tora of the main house.

TORA: Madam is here.

MOKUSUKE: What? She is? Oh, please come in!

> *Ofuji enters.*

OFUJI: Tell me, Mokusuke. Master is here isn't he?

MOKUSUKE: Yes. No. He is not here.

TORA (*officiously*): What do you mean he isn't? He's been

[69]

away from home for all of three days. Where else could he go? Out with it!

MOKUSUKE: But I've told you the truth. He is not here.

OFUJI (*placatingly*): Well, if you say so, I won't argue with you. But listen, Mokusuke, I am worried about him. He has hardly finished making the round of New Year's visits when he decides to stay out and not come home. Now I haven't enough to do, and the house seems deserted. I have a favor to ask of you. Can you see your way to granting it?

MOKUSUKE: Well, I can't say until you tell me what it is.

OFUJI: Well, the favor I have in mind is....

> *She takes his hand. Mokusuke is shocked*
> *by this intimacy and frees himself.*

MOKUSUKE (*righteously*): No, I can't grant you that favor.

OFUJI: Why not?

MOKUSUKE: Isn't it obvious? I am a poor servant earning only two gold pieces and two silver pieces a year. I've just put in a year's service. Until I put in three years faithfully, I won't be earning seven gold pieces and two silver. How can you ask me to be your lover?

TORA (*shocked*): Don't be impertinent! Why should Madam suggest such a thing?

MOKUSUKE (*relieved*): Oh! She doesn't want me for her lover? Well, then, I will listen to her request.

> *Ofuji wraps a coin in paper.*

OFUJI: This is only a trifle, Mokusuke. It's a New Year's gift from me. Buy yourself some tobacco with it.

> *He unwraps the paper.*

MOKUSUKE (*beside himself*): Oh! One silver piece! What

will I do with all the tobacco this will buy? I get mine for eight coppers.

TORA (*exasperated*): What a clod you are! It doesn't make any difference what you buy with it. It's a present from Madam.

MOKUSUKE: Then I will remit this to my home in the country. (*Suspiciously.*) It couldn't be counterfeit, though, could it?

TORA: Do you think for a moment that Madam would give you a counterfeit coin?

MOKUSUKE: Being too generous raises my suspicions.

OFUJI (*matter-of-factly*): Well, Mokusuke, my request shouldn't surprise you. Tell me truthfully: since when has my husband been here?

MOKUSUKE: All right, I'll tell. My lips were sealed, but your gift compels me to speak. The truth is that he has been here the day before yesterday, and oh, my, I have never seen such goings-on! Why, even before sundown they....

He stops after glancing at Ofuji.

TORA (*urging him on*): There's no need for niceties at a time like this. Speak frankly.

MOKUSUKE (*peevishly*): They're going to grind me down to a fine powder with their demands. It's "Go to Yao-han for special dishes." "Go to the bean-curd shop." "We're all out of wine." It's a feat every night.

TORA: What a burden to be used like that. After they have wine, Master and she....

MOKUSUKE: Yes, he and the mistress....

TORA: Oh, you make me angry! Call her "the doxy"!

MOKUSUKE: The doxy and Master....

[71]

TORA (*consumed with prurient curiosity*): Do what?

MOKUSUKE (*casually*): I think I'll have some tobacco first.

He smokes. Tora turns to Ofuji.

TORA: Madam, did you hear that? Doesn't that infuriate you?

OFUJI: Izayoi was once a prostitute. She must be familiar with what men call "techniques."

TORA: Oh, the more I hear the angrier I get. What did I tell you, Madam? You are put in such a position because, despite my advice, you have not complained, talking about a woman's place and woman's modesty. I'm vexed on your account!

> *She seizes Mokusuke by his collar and flings him about.*

MOKUSUKE: Oh, watch out! You'll crush my adam's apple! Let me go! Let me go!

TORA: All right, I will, but go on with your story.

MOKUSUKE: There is no more to tell.

TORA: Even you dare make fools of us! Master is also a fool! Why is he so stuck on the other one? You'd think they were two prawns fried in batter!

MOKUSUKE: I can't say I blame him. Madam and mistress are like a mud-turtle and the moon.

TORA: You mean me, don't you? I am the mud-turtle.

OFUJI (*calmly*): You needn't defend me, Tora. Even in Mokusuke's eyes Izayoi is as different from me as the moon is from a mud-turtle. I don't think my husband's infatuation is unreasonable. But when he does not come home, it is the duty of the wife to remonstrate, even if it hurts his feelings, for the sake of the family.

TORA (*egging her on*): Don't hold anything back now.

[72]

OFUJI (*uneasily*): But if I did speak out people will secretly call me a terrible, jealous woman.

TORA: But you must speak up.

OFUJI: Anyway, everything in its own good time. Mokusuke, lend us your room for a while.

MOKUSUKE: If you don't mind a filthy place, hide there.

OFUJI: We won't mind, Mokusuke.

MOKUSUKE: Very well, Madam.

> *Ofuji looks toward the interior of the house.*

OFUJI (*with fury*): Oh, the more I think of it....

> *Then she controls herself.*

OFUJI: Show us the way, Mokusuke.

> *The three exit toward the left of the anteroom. Music. The stage revolves, and the next scene follows immediately.*

IV. 2

Time: immediately following.

> *The scene: an interior. The set is raised off the stage floor. Upstage center are an alcove with a writing table and a chest of drawers on its right. There are sliding doors papered with silver foil and decorated with ink paintings. At stage left is an apartment fitted with paper sliding doors, with a stone wash basin in front. Next to it is a bamboo fence with grass, a plum tree, and a rustic garden gate. On both sides, at stage rear, a fence of split bamboo is visible. Hakuren and his three guests are seated at a banquet. Large*

[73]

trays, platters, and bowls are set out. The maid Yone is pouring wine. Music is played until the revolving stage comes to rest.

HEMPUKU: By the way, Hakuren, I have brought along a friend of mine who is very keen on haiku.

HAKUREN: I am very glad you did. Please consider me your friend.

GINSHICHI: I hope you will be as kind to me as you have been to Hempuku.

HAKUREN: And what is your name?

GINSHICHI (*flustered*): Well, uh, it's Takara Kikakui.

HAKUREN (*surprised*): What? You? The famous haiku poet?

HEMPUKU (*annoyed*): No, no. He means that he is a disciple of Takarai Kikaku.

GINSHICHI: Yes, and I call myself Marui Shikaku after my master.

HAKUREN: That's an unusual name, isn't it? Round Square.

SANJI (*musingly*): But it doesn't fit him, does it? Look at his face. It is long and dented in the middle—like a spoon.

YONE (*laughing*): You look like the actor Kichiroku.

GINSHICHI (*upset*): You are sticking the wrong label on me.

HEMPUKU (*in an undertone*): That's enough.

SANJI: By the way, what has happened to Izayoi?

HEMPUKU: You're right. She is taking a long time.

GINSHICHI: I am very anxious to make her acquaintance.

HAKUREN: She is probably still reading some new books that Yasaburō, the book dealer, brought recently.

YONE: Yes, she said she would read two or three more pages.

GINSHICHI: She could not put the book down, eh? It couldn't be a new erotic book, could it? My, uh, interest is aroused.

HEMPUKU: Now don't start on your boorish puns.

HAKUREN: Well, he seems quite an expert, probably under your guidance.

HEMPUKU: I'm embarrassed.

> *Izayoi enters to samisen music. She is dressed in the gaudy robes of a concubine.*

IZAYOI: Welcome, gentlemen.

HEMPUKU: Ah, Izayoi, you are as beautiful as always!

IZAYOI (*shyly*): Don't tease me, Hempuku.

> *She sits down next to Hakuren.*

SANJI: Say, Izayoi, I met the matron of the Ōgiya in the bazaar in front of the Asakusa Temple a few days ago. She told me you were the only thing they were talking about at the house. Well, you know what a garrulous old crone she is. I could not get away from her. |I stood prepared. But have more wine from a freshly-warmed there cornered.

IZAYOI: The next time you run into her, tell her to come and see me.

SANJI: She said she would when she visits the Katō Shrine.

HEMPUKU: By the way, Izayoi, let me introduce a friend to you.

GINSHICHI: My name is Marui Shikaku. I hope we will be friends.

IZAYOI: I hope so, too.

YONE: Come, gentlemen, whose cup needs refilling?

HEMPUKU: I have had enough.

IZAYOI (*apologetically*): I am afraid the meal was poorly prepared. But have more wine from a just-warmed bottle.

GINSHICHI: No, no more; and I am not just saying it out of politeness.

HAKUREN: Well, if that is the case, how about a poem from you?

GINSHICHI (*squirming*): I don't like to say no to my host, but I am a little indisposed tonight.

HEMPUKU (*sharply*): Don't give yourself such airs. Let us have a poem.

> *He gets the writing table and sets it down in front of Ginshichi.*

GINSHICHI (*trapped*): Oh, what a situation!

> *He struggles awkwardly at the table.*

HEMPUKU: Quickly, Master Shikaku. The opening haiku of the series.

GINSHICHI: Oh, all right!

> *He thinks hard.*

GINSHICHI: Two gold pieces in silver coins at the most!
> *Hempuku tugs at Ginshichi's sleeve.*

HEMPUKU (*nonplussed*): Here, now, that doesn't come out to seventeen syllables!

> *Ginshichi is thrown off course by figures.*

[76]

GINSHICHI: Seventeen ounces? Your appraisal is off. It is too high.

HAKUREN (*lost*): What is all this? What does he mean by "high"?

HEMPUKU (*covering*): He is referring to the high price of the set of poems by nine of Master Bashō's ten disciples. They were on sale recently.

SANJI: A set of nine? What a treasure!

HEMPUKU (*impressed*): I misjudged you, Sanji. To know about the ten disciples shows some refinement.

HAKUREN: It will soon be spring, won't it, Hempuku?

GINSHICHI: How about a cup, Master Ten Disciples?

He holds a cup out to Sanji.

SANJI: A cup? I am much obliged. This is like going to a flower-viewing picnic before the season.

IZAYOI: Hakuren, take me to see the wisteria at Kameido and the irises at Kinegawa this year.

HAKUREN: Certainly. Let us take Sanji along and spend the whole day.

SANJI: Did you say Kameido? I would enjoy that.

GINSHICHI: What about the Azuma Shrine behind the Tenjin Shrine?

SANJI: Mention Tenjin and you remind me of a hand in the flower card game.

HEMPUKU: It would be too bad if it rained.

SANJI: Don't mention rain. In cards, the "rain card" cancels out the "flower cards."

Hempuku's mind is still on haiku.

HEMPUKU: I am confused.

GINSHICHI: The iris season comes a little later, doesn't it?

[77]

SANJI: Did I hear iris mentioned? Shall we play a hand?

HEMPUKU: Let me break in a moment, Sanji. I know that the word "iris" is appropriate in haiku. But I don't know what "a hand" is.

SANJI: You are familiar with the game and you don't know what "a hand" means?

HEMPUKU (*earnestly*): In a haiku series there are rules about when a particular flower or the moon can be mentioned. But there are no rules about "a hand."

GINSHICHI: I never heard of it either.

HAKUREN: It seems to me that the "flowers" you two have in mind are not the same. Hempuku is thinking about haiku and Sanji about the card game. Better start all over again.

SANJI: Then we were on the wrong track all the way through?

YONE (*absent-mindedly*): Through with your meal, Sanji?

HAKUREN: You are on the wrong track again. Ha, ha, ha, ha!

Mokusuke enters.

MOKUSUKE: Master, Izayoi's father is here.

HAKUREN: Oh, is he?

IZAYOI: Show him into my room, Mokusuke.

MOKUSUKE: I have done just that.

HEMPUKU and GINSHICHI: We will be going, Hakuren.

SANJI: I will too.

HAKUREN: There is no need to go. Sanji, didn't you want to see me about something?

SANJI: I hate to ask you for it, but I need five gold pieces.

HAKUREN: What for?

SANJI: I have to make good some gambling losses. A fox tricked me.

IZAYOI: You give me the shivers! A fox tricked you?

HEMPUKU: What kind of fox was it that could have tricked you into such a large hole?

GINSHICHI (*slyly*): I think Sanji has another kind of hole in mind — a bigger one.

SANJI: We are off on the wrong track again.

HAKUREN: Well, no matter. Here you are. Don't overdo it.

> *He takes five gold pieces from his wallet, wraps it in paper, and gives it to Sanji.*

SANJI: I am grateful to you for this. Izayoi, please help me convey my thanks to Master.

> *Hakuren wraps two piles of coins in paper. Mokusuke interrupts.*

HAKUREN: I am very pleased that you two came to see me. I would like you to stay and do a series of haiku. But as you just heard, Izayoi's father just arrived, so let us do that some other time. This is not much, but use it to hire palanquins to get home.

> *He hands the money to Hempuku and Ginshichi.*

GINSHICHI: Oh, but this is only my first visit.

HEMPUKU: You show me the same kindness whenever I come. I am embarrassed to accept this.

HAKUREN: You need not be. I am going to ask you to judge my poems in the near future. Please accept this as payment in advance.

HEMPUKU: In that case, I will. Thank you very much. I

am anxious to read your poems. What about your
earlier collection?

Mokusuke interrupts.

MOKUSUKE: Well, let me tell you, the last cord of firewood
I collected was so green it wouldn't burn.

GINSHICHI: What's this nonsense? We're discussing a
different matter.

MOKUSUKE: Aren't we talking about firewood and cook-
ing?

IZAYOI: Mokusuke, you are wandering again.

YONE: Isn't he a fool?

MOKUSUKE (*sullenly*): What's so strange? He asked me
about the firewood I collected, and I told him it would
not burn.

HAKUREN (*dismissing him*): All right, all right. Tend to
your own business.

SANJI: By the way, gentlemen, are you going to Ōiso? If
you are, I will go with you.

HEMPUKU: Not to Ōiso but to Koiso to our favorite
house.

SANJI: You mean to the Ōyorozu? You sly rascals!

GINSHICHI: One thing we don't like about going there is
the smell from the charnel house we have to pass by.

*Mokusuke lifts the cover of the pan and
shouts.*

MOKUSUKE (*overjoyed*): Oh! The bones! The bones!
There is some left!

*Everyone shudders at the reference to
bones.*

ALL: Mokusuke, don't startle us so!

[80]

HAKUREN: It must be close to ten. If you are going to Koiso, the earlier the better.

HEMPUKU: You are right. Let us go right now. It is a deserted road.

GINSHICHI: It is not like going to Ōiso. The lonely fields are terrible to get through.

SANJI (*surprised*): But aren't you going to go by palanquin?

HEMPUKU (*matter of factly*): Nothing of the kind. How much do you think we would have left if we did that?

SANJI: You were given money for that purpose, but you are going to walk anyway, eh?

GINSHICHI (*in anticipation*): When I think of her I can go in my bare feet.

MOKUSUKE (*exasperated*): What greedy fellows!

HEMPUKU: Goodbye, Hakuren.

GINSHICHI: Goodbye, Izayoi.

IZAYOI: Have a good time.

HEMPUKU (*jokingly*): We are going to have a miserable time.

GINSHICHI: We're just going to make our partners happy.

HAKUREN: No doubt.

HEMPUKU and GINSHICHI: Ha, ha, ha, ha! Well, then, goodbye.

SANJI: Let's go.

> *To samisen music the three go down the runway. Mokusuke sees them off at the gate.*

MOKUSUKE: If I never see you again, that will be too soon!

YONE: Careful, they will hear you!

MOKUSUKE: What if they do?

HAKUREN: Stop mumbling, Mokusuke, and call Izayoi's father here.

MOKUSUKE: Very well, sir.

IZAYOI: Yone, will you put this place in order?

YONE: Yes, mistress.

> *She removes the wine bottles and the dishes.*

MOKUSUKE: Sagobei, please come in here.

> *Sagobei, who is now a priest, answers offstage.*

SAGOBEI (*subdued*): If you will excuse the instrusion.

> *Sagobei enters to melancholy samisen music. He is dressed as a priest, with a satchel hanging from his neck, coverings for the hands, leggings, and a bamboo basketwork hat in his hand. He goes to stage left and puts down the hat.*

SAGOBEI: Hakuren, I wish you a happy New Year.

HAKUREN: You are welcome, Sagobei. Don't stand on ceremony. Come closer.

SAGOBEI: Thank you.

IZAYOI: Father, it's good to see you again.

SAGOBEI: Ah, daughter, I see you are in good spirits. That is fine.

YONE: Please have some tea.

> *She pours tea and offers it to him.*

SAGOBEI: Don't go to any trouble for me. Like all old men, Hakuren, I keep saying the same things over and over again. It's about you and Izayoi. She has been my

[82]

support all these years. She sold herself into prostitution for my sake. The hardships of her life were too much for her. She escaped—and may the buddhas forgive her—attempted suicide in the Inase River. But by some miracle you rescued her. It was due to the intercession of the kind Amida who is full of pity. You told her that as life in the brothel was unbearable you would make it easier for her, and bought her out. You gave her a manservant and a maid. She has everything. She is a fortunate woman. I hope the gods will not punish her by taking her life away too soon. In good times or bad, it is the lot of the old to worry. How can I thank you enough for your kindnesses to me through my daughter? I pray to you every evening before my invocations to Amida.

He draws out his rosary and weeps.

HAKUREN (*deprecatingly*): There you go again. I wish you would stop. I would have saved anyone in that situation. That is my nature. I knew Izayoi. Would I have let her die? You need feel no obligation to me. Your fulsome thanks every time we meet embarrass me. Our relationships are all fixed in a previous existence.

IZAYOI: It has been a truly strange bond. You have been so kind to us since I came here a month ago. Please thank him warmly, father.

SAGOBEI: You don't have to tell me that. I cannot express my gratitude sufficiently.

He sheds tears of happiness.

SAGOBEI (*embarrassed*): In the old, tears are not far away from the surface, whether at sad or happy occasions.

He wipes away his tears.

MOKUSUKE (*realistically*): Doesn't your nose drip first?

YONE: You keep out of it.

[83]

SAGOBEI: That's all right. Mokusuke is right, you know.

HAKUREN: Why have you decided to become a priest?

SAGOBEI: I must pray for the repose of someone's soul.

IZAYOI: For whom, father?

SAGOBEI (*instinctively*): Your brother....

IZAYOI: What was that?

SAGOBEI (*covering*): I mean your mother, who died the year before last. I pray for her soul and spend all my time at devotions. Thanks to your charity I lack for nothing. All I do is visit holy places every day. It is an easy life.

IZAYOI: You are dressed for travel. Where are you going?

SAGOBEI: Since it is turning warm, I thought I would go on a pilgrimage to Zenkō Temple. I came to thank you and say goodbye.

HAKUREN: To Zenkō? That is commendable, but that area is known for its heavy snows. If I were you I would wait until the third month.

SAGOBEI: I expect they have cleared away most of the snow from the roads.

MOKUSUKE: That's what you think. When it comes to snow in my country, it doesn't start melting until the fifth month. When you cry or sniffle as you did just now, you will have icicles hanging from your face.

HAKUREN: There goes Mokusuke again with his exaggerated half-truths when he boasts about his native place. Ha, ha, ha , ha.

A bell tolls ten o'clock.

SAGOBEI: Is it ten already? I think I will be going.

IZAYOI: I hear it is unsafe in the streets these days. Stay overnight with us.

[84]

HAKUREN: Yes, you must. Start out from here tomorrow morning. It would be safer.

SAGOBEI: Then I will impose myself upon you.

YONE: You have made a wise decision.

SAGOBEI (*in a low voice*): Speaking about how unsafe it is outside, I hear that the thief they call "the Demon" has broken into several houses. And they still haven't arrested the robber who got into Paradise Temple last year and made off with the three thousand gold pieces that the shogun gave to the temple. He is a clever fellow, whoever he is.

> *Hakuren gives a guilty start. Mokusuke,*
> *the disguised magistrate, observes him.*

HAKUREN: I am sure the thief has got to Kyoto or Kyushu by now.

SAGOBEI: In any case, my advice to you is to be careful. You are rich.

IZAYOI: This talk makes me shiver.

MOKUSUKE (*enigmatically*): The thing about thieves is that there is no telling who is one.

HAKUREN: Eh?

MOKUSUKE (*innocently*): Oh, nothing. Well Sagobei, will you join me in a cup in the kitchen?

SAGOBEI (*relieved*): I would like nothing better. With you, I will not be so uncomfortable, and the wine will taste so much better.

MOKUSUKE: By the way, do you like duck bones?

SAGOBEI: No, I am observing a strict abstinence.

MOKUSUKE: Capital! Then I get them all.

SAGOBEI: Goodnight, Hakuren.

HAKUREN: Get a good night's rest.

SAGOBEI: Thank you for your hospitality.

> *Sagobei and Mokusuke exit to samisen music.*

YONE: It is already ten. Shall I lay out the bedding?

IZAYOI: Please do so. Hakuren, while Yone is getting our room ready, come sit by me.

HAKUREN (*not displeased*): You are in a hurry to get to bed, aren't you?

> *Yone goes into the apartment at stage left. Izayoi lights a pipe for Hakuren.*

HAKUREN: It's cold tonight. I think I will go to bed without changing.

IZAYOI: That's a good idea.

> *Yone enters.*

YONE: It is ready now.

> *Hakuren and Izayoi remove their cloaks, tie on narrow sashes, and prepare for bed. Yone bows to them.*

YONE: Good night.

> *She exits to samisen music.*

IZAYOI: Come, let us go to bed.

> *Izayoi rises. Hakuren looks at Izayoi.*

HAKUREN (*puzzled*): Am I mistaken, Izayoi, or is your waist thickening?

IZAYOI: Oh!

> *Startled, she conceals her waist with her sleeves.*

IZAYOI (*flustered*): I have never had a slim waist.

[86]

> *She avoids looking at Hakuren. They disappear into the bedroom, Hakuren looking doubtfully at Izayoi. Mokusuke enters and looks about. He stealthily lifts a short sword from its stand in the alcove, unsheaths it, and studies it intently by the light. He nods, slips it in the scabbard, and replaces it on the stand. He goes to stage right.*

MOKUSUKE (*as though to himself*): I was sure there was some wine left around here.

> *He looks around and exits. The time passes. A temple bell tolls the hour, and quiet samisen music is played. Izayoi comes out from the bedroom and throws a cloak over her shoulders. She rinses her hands at the stone basin in the garden. She brings out a memorial tablet, a rosary, and an incense burner from the chest of drawers and places them on the table. She pours water in a bowl and presses her hands together in prayer.*

IZAYOI: I pray that Seishin will attain buddhahood and nirvana. Hail to Amida Buddha. Hail to Amida Buddha.

> *She prays. Hakuren spies on her through the apartment door. Simultaneously, Ofuji watches her from the interior.*

HAKUREN (*brusquely*): Why the prayers, Izayoi?

IZAYOI: Oh!

> *She is startled, and attempts to put away the devotional objects.*

HAKUREN (*calmly*): There is no need to do that.

[87]

IZAYOI: But....

HAKUREN: You have my permission.

> *He enters the room.*

IZAYOI: Forgive me.

> *She breaks down and weeps.*

HAKUREN: Every night, after you made sure I was asleep, you have been slipping out of bed to pray for someone's soul. Who is it—your mother, brother, or someone you promised to be true to while you were in the quarter? Be frank with me.

> *Hakuren lights a pipe.*

IZAYOI: I have kept this from you, but now that you know, there is no reason to conceal it any longer. I will tell you everything.

> *Samisen music with Chinese fiddle is played.*

IZAYOI: This tablet is for the man I promised to love in this world and the next. His name was Seishin and he was a monk. He was arrested for going to the quarter and was banished. I was then with his child. I knew I could not be at the brothel very long and escaped. I was desperate. I made up my mind to die with him—to make our way over the Hill of the Dead and the Sanzu River—since we could not be together in this world. We threw ourselves into the Inase River. You saved me. You paid off my debt to the quarter. I cannot repay you for your kindness, or for your charity to my father. I thought that the least I could do to requite such generosity was to conceal my condition and serve you in the bedchamber. Since you had spent a fortune on my account, I was yours to do with as you pleased. But in my heart all the time I was as a nun, loyal to the dead Seishin. And for the day when I wouldr ask you fo

permission to make a pilgrimage to various temples in
the country, I made myself a set of nuns' robes. Here
they are.

> *She takes out from a drawer a white
> undergarment, a black robe, shields for
> the hands, and leggings. Ofuji weeps.
> Hakuren is touched. He puts down his
> pipe.*

HAKUREN: I am moved by your fidelity. How true the
words of that Shinnai tune are: "I was blind to facts
when I said that in the hearts of courtesans there was
no sincerity. They were the words of a churl and a fool."
I do not know what kind of man Seishin was, but he is
fortunate to be so loved. How unhappy you must have
been to sleep with me out of a sense of duty. I feel no
desire for you now. I will act like a man: I give you
permission to go.

IZAYOI (*unbelieving*): Am I free to go?

HAKUREN: You are indeed. When you become a nun,
spend all your time in prayer for your husband.

IZAYOI: Oh, thank you.

> *Sagobei enters, wiping away tears.*

SAGOBEI: I heard everything from the next room. We are
even deeper in your debt now. How can I express my
gratitude?

HAKUREN: Money is to be had for the asking, but this
fidelity is not to be bought for all the money in the
world.

SAGOBEI: She is undeserving of such praise. Izayoi, you
are too good to be a daughter of mine. How happy
Seishin must be in his grave!

IZAYOI: Now I can set out with head high. There is no

[89]

time like the present. I will cut off my hair and become a nun tonight.

SAGOBEI: A good idea. Seishin died on this same day though in another month. I cannot read the sutras, but I am dressed like a monk. I will shave your head for you.

IZAYOI: May I trouble you, father?

HAKUREN (*suddenly dismayed*): Then you are renouncing the world so soon?

IZAYOI: Since I have your permission, yes.

SAGOBEI: It has been her long-cherished desire to serve the Buddha.

HAKUREN: Still it is a pity to see you lose your glossy black hair.

SAGOBEI (*sadly*): When it is gone she will lose the symbol of her beauty.

IZAYOI (*with no regret*): But I will become a new nun, as fresh as the green willow tree.

HAKUREN: I wish you good health, my new nun.

IZAYOI: Hakuren....

HAKUREN: Izayoi....

> *They look at each other, full of emotion.*

SAGOBEI: Well then, I will apply the razor.

> *A song is sung offstage. Weeping, Sagobei takes Izayoi by the hand. Izayoi exits with the nun's garments. Ofuji breaks out in a sob. Hakuren is startled.*

HAKUREN: Who is that?

OFUJI: It is I.

HAKUREN: Ofuji? What are you doing here?

> *Ofuji enters.*

[90]

OFUJI (*remorsefully*): I came secretly this evening because you had deserted me. I came to take out my anger on the woman who had seduced you. But Izayoi's fidelity was something I had not expected. When I heard her speak of her determination to remain faithful to her lover and to become a nun at her tender age, my resentment vanished. Now I feel as though she were my niece or sister, and I cannot help but love her. Please forgive me for nagging you all this time. I did not know the circumstances.

HAKUREN (*ill at ease*): I think you had some justification for your jealous outbursts. But as you have gathered, she has few friends. This may sound like an excuse, but I was placed in a situation of having to look after her when I saved her life. It was not only because of sexual passion on my part. You can be sure that I will leave this house and spend all my time at home from now on.

Tora enters.

TORA (*triumphant*): How happy you must be, Madam. With the doxy a baldpated nun, the situation is well in hand. I am so glad for you I can hardly contain myself.

OFUJI: What's this? What has come over you? I do not want Izayoi to overhear you and think I agree with you. I could not face her. Be a little more prudent in what you say.

TORA (*puzzled*): I do not understand, Madam. Did you not say to me, "Tora, speak out for me as I am too timid to do so."?

OFUJI: Why must you insist on speaking? Be quiet!

TORA: But you said....

OFUJI: You will still talk back to your mistress, will you? Hakuren, our maid is most impertinent. Let us dismiss her in the third month.

[91]

TORA: What have I done wrong?

Mokusuke and Yone enter.

MOKUSUKE (*tearfully*): Master, master! My mistress has become a nun. What a pity! I do not think there will be another like her. I am clumsy, and Master is always after me. But mistress intercedes for me all the time. Not only that, but she offers me all of the left-over wine and dishes. I know she is going on a pilgrimage, but that does not console me.

YONE: I am just as sorrowful as Mokusuke here. I am so stupid, yet mistress used to tell me to do things for her and was kind to me.

MOKUSUKE: You are sad, too, are you? I am heartbroken.

They weep.

HAKUREN: I understand your feelings. I may seem to be without feelings, but even if I do not weep as you do, I am every bit as melancholy. I have felt regret at parting from a woman I was not especially fond of. Think what it is like in Izayoi's case.

He glances at Ofuji and stops.

HAKUREN: You must not take offence, Ofuji. Ha, ha, ha, ha!

Sagobei speaks offstage.

SAGOBEI: You are ready now, daughter. Come quickly.

> *Sagobei enters, followed by Izayoi in a nun's black habit and light-blue head covering. She goes to stage right, sits down, and looks down shyly.*

SAGOBEI: I have turned her into a nun, Hakuren.

IZAYOI (*gratefully*): Thanks to you, Hakuren, I have abandoned the world.

> *They all look at Izayoi and weep.*

HAKUREN: Ofuji, look: in the twinkling of an eye, and without regret, she has renounced the world.

OFUJI: I was moved by your confession and your desire to become a nun.

IZAYOI: Those words are like a balm for someone you should resent.

SAGOBEI: This looks like a good time to make my request.

Madam, what would you think of becoming a sister to Izayoi?

OFUJI (*eagerly*): Nothing would please me more. Let us not delay a minute. We shall exchange wine cups here and now.

SAGOBEI and IZAYOI: You do not object?

OFUJI: Tora, bring me a wine cup.

TORA: Yes, Madam.

> *She brings a wine cup and a bottle. Ofuji takes up the cup.*

OFUJI: Since I am the elder, I will drink first.

> *She holds out the cup. Tora pours. Ofuji drinks and hands the cup to Izayoi. Izayoi drinks from it.*

IZAYOI: May I offer you the cup in return?

> *She hands it to Ofuji, who drinks from it.*

OFUJI: This makes us sisters from today.

SAGOBEI: My wish has been granted.

SAGOBEI and IZAYOI: Thank you.

[93]

IZAYOI: Oh, here are some things I would like to give you for services rendered, and also as keepsakes.

> *She brings out from under her collar a hairpin wrapped in paper which she gives to Yone, and a comb which she gives to Tora.*

IZAYOI: They are old but still usable. I have nothing that a man can use, so to Mokusuke I give a small amount.

> *She hands him a packet of money.*

YONE: A keepsake? You are most kind.

TORA (*dumfounded*): For me, too? I do not deserve this.

MOKUSUKE: You should not have done this. Money again. Should I buy tobacco?

YONE: Anything you like. It is a parting gift from mistress.

MOKUSUKE: Thank you....

MOKUSUKE, YONE, TORA: ...very much!

IZAYOI: When you think of me say a prayer for me.

> *Mokusuke, Yone, and Tora burst into tears.*

SAGOBEI: Come, daughter, we must go.

HAKUREN: Wait a moment, old man. You two are starting out on a pious journey. Let me give you a trifling parting gift.

> *He takes some coins from his purse, wraps them up, and gives them to Sagobei.*

SAGOBEI: But I cannot....

HAKUREN: It will be a long journey and you will need travelling expenses.

SAGOBEI: You think of everything.

SAGOBEI and IZAYOI: Thank you.

[94]

OFUJI: I can only offer you rice with red beans on a happy occasion like this. Won't you consider starting out after a ceremony tomorrow morning?

IZAYOI: You are very kind, but I would be embarrassed at being seen.

OFUJI: I hear that you are pregnant. I will be anxious about you. When you settle down somewhere, send me news.

IZAYOI: I promise I will.

SAGOBEI: Well then, daughter.

IZAYOI, SAGOBEI: May you all be in good health.

HAKUREN: You too.

MOKUSUKE: We will wait for....

HAKUREN, OFUJI, et al: ...your return to Kamakura.

> *Sagobei and Izayoi step down and start for the gate. A temple bell tolls.*

SAGOBEI (*solemnly*): We now leave you to start a long pilgrimage.

IZAYOI (*sadly*): This may be a parting forever.

HAKUREN: I think of a fragile cherry blossom and its cruel fate.

MOKUSUKE: I think of it in full bloom.

OFUJI: Even without a wind in the night....

IZAYOI: ...it will scatter in all directions, just as I, in my black robe, will wander.

SAGOBEI: Show Hakuren how you have changed.

> *He slips off Izayoi's head covering and reveals her shaven head.*

HAKUREN: Admirable!

[95]

He and Izayoi look at each other.

IZAYOI: Oh!

She is embarrassed and covers her head with Sagobei's hat of woven bamboo. At this cue, the clappers are struck.

IZAYOI: I am ashamed!

Izayoi peers at Hakuren from under the hat. Hakuren, deeply touched, turns to Ofuji. They all freeze in a tableau. To the tolling of the hour of dawn, the cawing of crows, and samisen music, the curtain is drawn.

ACT SIX SCENE ONE

Time: One year later. Evening.

The scene: the interior of Hakuren's residence at Yukinoshita. The house is raised off the stage floor on a riser of clay and plaited bamboo. The central room is fitted with paper sliding doors and an openwork transom. Upstage center is a an arched doorway with a recessed cupboard to its left and a brown wall with a papered skirt to its right. At stage left is an apartment with sliding walls of paper on wooden grills. There is a roofed gate. At downstage right is an entrance hall nine feet wide with a wooden door. Near it is hung a large paper lantern emblazoned with a family crest. The curtain is drawn to lively music. Nihachi, a noodle vendor, is setting down his small hand-lantern, and behind him, Donshichi and Kanroku, friends from neighboring tenements, are putting their gong and drum on the ground.

NIHACHI: Is anybody at home?

DONSHICHI and KANROKU: Anybody home?

NIHACHI: Nobody seems to be in.

DONSHICHI: It looks as though they havn't replaced your daughter Tora after she disappeared over two nights ago.

KANROKU: These people must be very shorthanded right now.

NIHACHI: Anyway, let us try once more.

NIHACHI, DONSHICHI, KANROKU: Anybody home?

> *Mokusuke says "Coming!" and enters from the interior.*

MOKUSUKE: Oh, it's Nihachi, Tora's father.

NIHACHI: Ah, Mokusuke. I must apologize to you. You must be working twice as hard since Tora ran off.

MOKUSUKE: Well, let me tell you! I am having a time of it because of Tora. From the time I jump up in the morning until I fall into bed at night, I wash and cook the rice, fetch the water, do the shopping, and run errands. It's Mokusuke this and Mokusuke that for everything. I do the work of two servants but only get the wages and food for one. It's unfair!

NIHACHI (*plaintively*): If I could, I would do something for your pains. But what can a noodle vendor do? As it is I have a hard time laying in supplies, and when I run into a spell of bad weather, I can barely earn three coppers.

DONSHICHI: It's all Tora's fault, worrying her father and inconveniencing her master.

KANROKU: That isn't all. She has made her neighbors go searching for her with gong and drum.

[98]

MOKUSUKE: Have you located her yet?

NIHACHI: We have searched for three days, but no luck. A man is involved. She must have eloped.

KANROKU (*disgusted*): Who would run off with such a homely girl?

NIHACHI: Mokusuke, you were with her from morning to night. Did you see anything suspicious?

MOKUSUKE (*thinking back*): Nothing unusual, but Izayoi —she used to be my master's mistress—has a father who is the keeper of a potter's field at Muen Temple in Nagoshi. A gravedigger there is enthusiastic about chanting narratives from the puppet theatre. Every time Tora came back from an errand for Madam, she used to talk about his recitation. It may be that he is her lover. Why don't you go there and find out?

NIHACHI: You may have something there. I heard that Izayoi became a nun and went on a pilgrimage to the provinces. Has she returned?

MOKUSUKE: She and her father set out together, but I heard that Izayoi was kidnapped by a gang of ruffians on a back road in Hakone. The old man was crestfallen, but there was nothing for him to do but come back. Then he was hired as a grave keeper.

NIHACHI: I can well sympathize with him. I have lost a daughter, too. I am sure he does not sleep nights. Children are the cause of all our troubles.

> *Ofuji enters. She is dressed in the clothes of a married woman of some status.*

OFUJI: Oh, it's Tora's father. Good evening.

NIHACHI (*apologetically*): I hardly know what excuse to make for Tora. We still have not traced her. I am sorry for the inconvenience she has caused you.

[99]

OFUJI: Not at all. I do not mind being without help. But I hope for your sake that you find her soon. You must be worried.

NIHACHI (*dejectedly*): Imagine how I feel. This is the third day. My business is at a standstill. My savings are all gone. Now I will have a hard time getting started again. And all because of that unfilial wench.

> *Ofuji gets her purse from under her collar, takes some coins from it, and wraps them in paper.*

OFUJI: You certainly are having a hard time of it. This is only a pittance, but use it to buy supplies.

She gives him the money.

NIHACHI: I thank you for your generosity, but to accept this after all the trouble my daughter has caused you...

OFUJI: It is only a trifling amount. Think nothing of it.

NIHACHI: I do not feel I deserve it.

MOKUSUKE: She has given it to you. Buy yourself some tobacco with it.

NIHACHI: Thank you very much.

DONSHICHI: Well, then, let's go now and make a round over on the other side of the river.

KANROKU: Now that you have some money on you, how about a drink somewhere?

MOKUSUKE: You sly fox! You lost no time, didn't you?

NIHACHI: I will buy both of you some wine as a token of my appreciation.

DONSHICHI: I won't wait to be asked twice.

KANROKU: Let's be on our way.

MOKUSUKE: You tipplers!

OFUJI: Don't be rude!

NIHACHI: Goodbye, Madam.

OFUJI: Let me know when you have located her.

NIHACHI: I will.

The three go out through the gate.

NIHACHI, DONSHICHI, KANROKU: Tora! Where are you?

MOKUSUKE (*upset*): Do they have to yell right in front of our gate?

NIHACHI, DONSHICHI, KANROKU: Missing person! Missing person!

They go down the runway beating the gong and drum.

OFUJI (*annoyed*): Really, where is that troublesome girl? Doesn't she care about her father? By the way, didn't someone come by a while ago?

MOKUSUKE: Yes. Kojibei of the Iseya shop came and asked to borrow five more gold pieces, making it a total of ten.

OFUJI: So that was it.

MOKUSUKE: And four or five people from the theater came to say they were sorry but we would have to wait until opening day for the fifty gold pieces they borrowed under their joint signatures.

OFUJI: Very well. I will tell Master.

MOKUSUKE: Imagine my dismay! They paid nothing on the interest, and they smoked all the tobacco I served them. They acted as though they had a right to it. Even one silver coin's worth of tobacco would not last long with those rascals.

OFUJI: Don't say any more. If you run out of tobacco, I will get you some.

[101]

MOKUSUKE (*with feeling*): Thank you. But take my advice and do not loan money to theater people. Nobody is more underhanded.

OFUJI: Don't be so abusive. Take care you do not doze off.

MOKUSUKE: Very well.

> *Music and song, with drum and flute. Izayoi, with close-cropped hair under a kerchief and in everyday clothes, comes down the runway with Seishin, now the notorious thief, Seikichi. He is dressed in informal clothes with the hem of the outer garment tucked under his sash. He also has a kerchief over his head. They stop on the runway.*

SEIKICHI: Hey, Izayoi, where does the man who used to keep you live?

IZAYOI: Not so loud. His house is over there.

SEIKICHI (*musingly*): Hm. A nice house, with an official lantern in front. It must be a money-lending office.

IZAYOI: I never found out where he got it, but he does have a lot of money.

SEIKICHI: That's what I am after.

IZAYOI (*reflectively*): What brought us together again, do you think? I was so sure you were dead that I shaved my hair off. But look at me now: here I am with you again, and my hair is growing in. What do you make of this?

SEIKICHI: We are tied to each other for good or bad. I was banished on account of my visits to you. My hair grew longer, my money ran out, and then I changed my outlook on life completely. It is easy to fall into evil ways, and before long I had a handle to my name. Example is a good teacher they say, and you were soon doing your share—stealing clothes from bathhouses and doing a little blackmailing.

IZAYOI: I was a coward at first, but at your prodding, I have done my bit. But I do not deserve any credit for it. If my friends should hear of what I am doing, they would say, "Why does she do it?" When I think about that I am embarrassed.

SEIKICHI: It was the same with me. Blackmailers, swindlers, and burglars should have something sinister about them, like a humped nose or large, glittering eyes. But I am short and hardly worth a second glance, with hair just barely grown in at that. It is only with pluck that I pull off my jobs. We have been fated to be together. Let us give each other a helping hand and do our best.

IZAYOI: Well, then, for a starter, let me try working on Hakuren.

SEIKICHI: Do you want me to come, too?

IZAYOI: No, you wait at the gate. I will handle the preliminaries.

SEIKICHI: You sound like a real professional now.

> *They come to the stage. Ofuji is reading a book by a lamp. Mokusuke is dozing. Izayoi whispers something to Seikichi.*

IZAYOI: Is anybody home?

OFUJI: Wake up, Mokusuke. There is someone at the door.

MOKUSUKE: Aye.

> *He is startled out of his sleep and jumps up.*

MOKUSUKE: Yes, yes. Here I come.

> *He rubs his eyes and opens the gate.*
> *Izayoi bows low.*

MOKUSUKE (*gruffly*): If it is charity you are after, come tomorrow before ten.

IZAYOI (*humbly*): No, I am not here for charity. I want to see Master or Madam.

MOKUSUKE (*peremptorily*): Don't be absurd. I said there will be no more handouts today. Go away, go away.

IZAYOI: Please don't say that and....

MOKUSUKE (*cruelly*): You obstinate creature! I said move on!

> *He shoves Izayoi away from the gate.*

IZAYOI (*bristling*): What are you doing, Mokusuke? Don't be so rough with me!

MOKUSUKE (*not impressed*): What? You know my name? That's a fine thing. Do you think I have acquaintances among beggars?

IZAYOI: As though you didn't.

> *She slips off her kerchief. Mokusuke is*
> *astonished.*

MOKUSUKE: Oh, it's Izayoi! Madam, Izayoi has come back!

OFUJI: What, Izayoi back?
> *She gets up.*

OFUJI: How glad I am to see you. Come in, come in.

IZAYOI: I humbly beg your pardon, my lady.

> *Izayoi bows and enters. She settles her-*
> *self wretchedly at stage right.*

OFUJI: Well, tell me what happened. We were very much

concerned. As we had no word from you, my husband and I often talked about you.

IZAYOI: That is very kind of you. I became separated from my father during the journey and fell into the hands of a gang of ruffians. I had a terrible time.

OFUJI: Is that what happened? It's no wonder you have changed so.

MOKUSUKE: Is it any wonder that I did not recognize you at first?

OFUJI: You were pregnant then. Where did you deliver the child?

IZAYOI: I gave birth in the mountains, but as I had little milk, I had to put it out to nurse.

OFUJI: I am relieved to hear that you had your child. Was it a boy or a girl?

IZAYOI: It was a boy.

OFUJI: Ah, how very fortunate! How happy your father will be when he learns about this. I can't wait to send word to him.

IZAYOI: I have not seen my father yet. Does he come here?

MOKUSUKE: He has been here quite frequently.

IZAYOI: Is that so? I have not seen him since we became separated. I was wondering where he was. I did not even know whether he was alive or not.

MOKUSUKE: He is in charge of the potter's field at Muen Temple.

IZAYOI: Now I know where he is. I shall go and see him as soon as I can.

OFUJI: You would do well to do that. I cannot tell you how worried he is.

[105]

IZAYOI: The more I think about it the more I realize how unfilial I have been.

OFUJI: You still have a long life ahead of you to make up for it.

IZAYOI: Thank you. By the way, is your husband at home?

OFUJI: Yes, he is taking a nap in the back.

IZAYOI (*diffidently*): May I ask a favor of you?

OFUJI: Why the sudden formality, Izayoi? We are as good as sisters. Speak up.

IZAYOI (*hesitantly*): I have no place to stay in Kamakura. If it will not inconvenience you, I would like to stay here. A corner in the kitchen or some such place will do for me.

OFUJI: Why of course. Your father lives in the compound of a temple so they probably would not allow a woman to live there. From this moment, think of this as your home.

IZAYOI: You are very kind.

OFUJI (*in a bantering tone*): But when I think of the past, I get a little worried. Ha, ha, ha.

IZAYOI: I am sure you are teasing me. I have something more to ask: could you put up another person?

OFUJI: Is he your companion?

IZAYOI: Yes.

OFUJI: Where is he?

IZAYOI: At the gate.

OFUJI: Why didn't you bring him in with you? Mokusuke, go and call him in.

MOKUSUKE: Very well.

He goes to the gate.

MOKUSUKE: Are you Izayoi's companion?

SEIKICHI: Yes, I am.

MOKUSUKE (*under his breath*): My, how evil he looks! Come in, come in.

SEIKICHI: Thank you.

> *He slips off his head covering. When he enters Ofuji is startled by his appearance and is ill at ease.*

OFUJI (*uneasily*): Then you are....

SEIKICHI: Yes, I am her companion.

OFUJI: Mokusuke, go and call your master.

MOKUSUKE: Aye.

> *He starts to rise. Hakuren calls out from within.*

HAKUREN: No need to come. I will be there in a moment.

> *Hakuren enters. He wears a black hood and an overcoat. He carries a tobacco tray holding a tobacco container and a pipe.*

HAKUREN: Well, Izayoi, I see you are back. It has been a long time, hasn't it?

IZAYOI: It is good to see you again. You are in good spirits as usual.

HAKUREN: Yes.

> *He sits down.*

HAKUREN: You are looking well. Good health is a blessing.

IZAYOI: Thank you. Your wife has just told me that my father has been coming here and causing you no end of trouble.

[107]

HAKUREN: It is hardly any trouble.

OFUJI: Izayoi has just asked for permission to stay with us. I agreed, but she also has this companion. What shall I do?

MOKUSUKE: The fewer parasites the better. I will have a time of it preparing the meals.

HAKUREN: Hold your tongue and don't meddle!

He turns to Seikichi.

HAKUREN: You are Izayoi's companion?

SEIKICHI: Yes. Then you must be Hakuren. This is the first time we have met. I hope we will be friends.

HAKUREN: Izayoi, is he a relative of yours?

IZAYOI: Yes, he is my...husband.

HAKUREN: What, your husband?

OFUJI: Then you are married, Izayoi?

MOKUSUKE: Whoever said that husband and wife get to resemble each other was right. Look they both have shaven heads.

HAKUREN: Anyway, you have settled down. That is good.

SEIKICHI: I know it is an imposition on you, but I hope you will let me stay here with my wife.

HAKUREN: Well, that depends. What is your name?

SEIKICHI: Since your wife and Izayoi are sworn sisters, you and I are as good as brothers. That being the case, I will conceal nothing from you.

> *He rolls up his left sleeve and reveals a thistle tattooed on his arm.*

SEIKICHI (*threateningly*): I am Seikichi, the thief with the tattoo on his arm. Sometimes they call me "the Demon Priest" because I was once a monk.

[108]

Everyone except Izayoi gives a start.

HAKUREN: What? Then the priest Seishin who was Izayoi's lover has become the notorious Seikichi?

SEIKICHI: Right.

OFUJI: What do you do?

SEIKICHI: Being an idler by nature, I don't have an honorable profession. I blackmail, swindle, and steal—in plain words, a robber. Practice makes perfect, they say, and Izayoi helps along nicely by lifting things from bathhouses.

> *His gestures and tone of voice become increasingly sinister.*

IZAYOI: Here, now, don't say such things in front of my sister. She'll worry.

SEIKICHI: You're right. Madam, you are indeed fortunate in having such a nice young sister.

MOKUSUKE: Then you are thieves—both of you!

SEIKICHI: Not so loud! I ask you—would you take us for anything else? But supposing someone heard you? I would have a rope around me before I could turn around. If that should happen, I will say that this was my hideout and you are my accomplices.

MOKUSUKE: But to be taken in by a couple of thieves....

HAKUREN: Mokusuke, keep out of this and be quiet!

MOKUSUKE: Aye!

> *Mokusuke watches Seikichi.*

IZAYOI: Sister, may I have a puff?

OFUJI: Yes. I think there is a pipe around here.

> *She searches*

IZAYOI: If you don't have one, I will ask Hakuren to lend me his.

HAKUREN: Here you are.

> *He hands her the tobacco jar and pipe.*

IZAYOI (*recollecting*): This is the pipe I used every night. It reminds me of those days.

> *She draws on it and then holds it out to Hakuren.*

IZAYOI (*brazenly*): Would you like a puff?

SEIKICHI (*annoyed*): What do you mean by offering a pipe to another man in front of your husband? Stop that foolishness!

IZAYOI: You keep quiet. I am trying to wheedle seven gold pieces and two silver coins out of him for you.

SEIKICHI (*sneeringly*): Why, that's next to nothing in repayment for the advantages he took of you. I have brooded over how I could personally thank him, and here I am at last. I was foolhardy and rash when I jumped into the river with this woman, but it was her luck to get snagged in your net. You saved her and bought her out from the brothel. You took care of her father. In exchange for all that, you kept her in a house in Hase Lane and enjoyed her every night. In the end you turned her into a nun and threw her out—and all in the name of kindness. You told her to go around praying for my soul. To soothe your conscience as her sworn sister you gave her some money for her journey, but it was consolation money. If that was not abuse, what would you call it? She has a lot to thank you for.

HAKUREN (*taken aback*): I do not think I deserve that. I don't know what Izayoi has told you, but when she told me she was going to become a nun and remain faithful to you, I thought it was admirable in a harlot.

I had paid a high price for her release, but I agreed and let her go. Say what you will, I believe I have acted like a man.

IZAYOI: Indeed! You can find an excuse for anything. Listening to you, anyone would think that was true.

Ofuji is upset by this.

OFUJI: What do you mean by saying "you can find an excuse for anything?" The requests to become a nun and to exchange wine cups as sworn sisters came from you and your father. That is why I agreed. Surely you could not have forgotten that?

MOKUSUKE: That reminds me: I still remember that occasion. Madam gave me one silver coin earlier in the evening for tobacco, and Izayoi gave me another as a parting gift. I have three all told wrapped up in my loin cloth. If you think I am lying, I will show you.

Izayoi ignores him and turns to Ofuji.

IZAYOI: Come, sister, I am surprised you can say such things. You got me to shave my hair off with your talk about the afterlife. You told me to go on a pilgrimage to pray for Seishin's soul. You assumed a false face and agreed to become my sister. You told me I could come to you in time of need, and then you threw me out. What was your motive? Jealousy. You have no idea what I went through, thanks to you. I may be a simple woman, but I will not put up with your lies.

OFUJI (*shocked*): What has got into you? What reason did I have to encourage you to become a nun?

IZAYOI: You don't fool me. You made me do it because you were jealous.

OFUJI: I deny that I ever encouraged you to....

[111]

IZAYOI: Yes, you did. It was you who turned me into a nun!

She raises her voice.

SEIKICHI: You're too loud. Lower your voice. Don't be vulgar, Izayoi. You are acting like a blackmailer or a swindler. Keep your voice down.

HAKUREN: Ofuji, you keep out of this, too.

OFUJI: But. . . .

HAKUREN: What good is your talking to them?

SEIKICHI (*with mock sweetness*): Have the goodness to forgive her, elder sister. It is only because you are sisters that she feels she can argue about foolish matters. We are going to depend on your kindness indefinitely. But we don't intend to sit around doing nothing. We will answer the door for you.

IZAYOI: You are right. With this cropped head I will feel I got the short end unless you make up to me, Hakuren. You don't look very happy. I suppose I don't appeal to you any more. But when I was your mistress, you did not mind going to bed with me. Wipe away that grim look and give me a smile.

> *She pulls the kerchief off her shoulder and flaps it against Hakuren's face. Ofuji is ruffled.*

OFUJI: Don't be impertinent!

MOKUSUKE: Don't do anything rash.

He restrains Ofuji.

HAKUREN: I have heard you out. I have done favors for you in the past, and I consent to your staying. But I run a money-lending office as you can see. You could not answer the door the way you look now. Come back after your hair has grown back to normal. Then I will allow you to stay. I will keep my word.

SEIKICHI: Huh! I am running out of patience. In my circle no one thinks about tomorrow. Today may be our last day. Do you think we have time to waste while our hair grows in—and just so that we can stay here?

IZAYOI: Are you afraid to put us up because of our appearance? There is no need to be frightened. We are sworn sisters, but if worse comes to worse, I have the upper hand. One word from me, and you are involved. If you do anything to cross me, I will implicate you.

SEIKICHI: Hey, don't use words like "involved" or "implicate." They are out of date. Nobody uses them these days. I could leave your house, Hakuren, and live like a rich retired man with all the fine things of life. But to be on the run is something I do not relish. This is my true feeling, so set your mind at rest and put us up. But if, as you say, we would make poor doorkeepers, we will disappear for a while, so please lend us some money.

HAKUREN: Very well. If it is your decision to go on a trip, I will give you enough to provide yourselves with sandals. I will make it a gift.

IZAYOI: That is what I call friendship. I hope you will be generous.

HAKUREN: I won't know how much you have in mind unless I ask. How much do you want?

SEIKICHI: We have no idea where we are going. A small sum won't last very long. Make it a nice, round figure: a hundred gold coins.

OFUJI, MOKUSUKE: What? That much?

HAKUREN (*calmly*): Are you sure only a hundred will do?

SEIKICHI (*surprised*): Huh?

[113]

HAKUREN: That is not much. Ofuji, bring me the chest.

OFUJI: Very well.

> *She brings a chest from the closet.*
> *Hakuren releases the lock and takes out*
> *a packet of a hundred gold pieces.*

HAKUREN: There you are. A hundred gold pieces.

SEIKICHI (*incredulous*): I was hardly expecting this.

> *He picks up the packet.*

MOKUSUKE: Oh, a hundred gold pieces for sandals! What expensive sandals! I cannot believe my ears.

> *Seikichi and Izayoi are amazed. But*
> *Seikichi's attention is caught by the seal*
> *on the paper wrapper.*

SEIKICHI: What's this seal?

HAKUREN (*alarmed*): Eh?

SEIKICHI (*excitedly*): This is the mark of the seal of the Paradise Temple! Where did this money come from?

HAKUREN: Uh....

SEIKICHI: Your story ought to be an interesting one. With this kind of money around, I return the piddling hundred gold pieces.

> *He throws the packet to Hakuren.*

HAKUREN: How much do you want then?

SEIKICHI (*deliberately*): Three thousand gold pieces.

HAKUREN: What?

SEIKICHI: When I was the sexton at the temple, a masked thief broke in and made away with the three thousand gold pieces that Lord Yoritomo offered the temple in the name of his ancestors. The thief vanished, and suspicion fell on me. I was arrested and my visits to the brothel were exposed. I was exiled. Do you blame me for thinking of the thief as my enemy? I was beginning to think he led a charmed life, and no wonder. It would have taken a million years to uncover him. He was operating a lending office all this time, an office with a grand entrance and an official lantern. He was a retainer to royalty. I will wager that even the local magistrate investigating the robbery does not realize that a gentleman entitled to wear swords is a thief.

Hakuren remains silent.

IZAYOI (*the light dawns*): Well, well! Then it was you who stole the money from the temple. You had me fooled. I used to wonder where the money you spent came from. This is fine. You men are brothers under the skin. We are more intimate than ever. The men will work at night, and sister and I will work as best we can by robbing bathhouses.

Mokusuke has been fuming all the while.

MOKUSUKE: You unfrocked priest! You have given yourself the license to say any number of monstrous things. How dare you accuse my master of taking the money. What proof have you?

SEIKICHI: Be quiet, you fool! Would I have accused him without proof?

MOKUSUKE: Well, where is the evidence?

SEIKICHI: I will tell you: it was my duty to stamp the packets of money. To anyone else the seal is only an ordinary one with faint, undecipherable characters. But I have no trouble making it out. This is my proof. There is no doubt who is the thief. The evidence, this inch-long seal, is conclusive. I will vouch for it.

[115]

> *Mokusuke is convinced, but he acts hostile on purpose.*

MOKUSUKE: You are making up stories, accusing my master on the basis of some seal or other. If I turn you in, they will clear up the matter for us. I will bind you up and take you in to the authorities!

SEIKICHI (*challengingly*): This is interesting! I dare you. If you hand me over, we all go, strung together like beads on a rosary—this couple and you.

OFUJI (*losing her composure*): Oh! Nobody has ever said such a hateful thing to me before.

MOKUSUKE: You scoundrel! You will threaten us, will you?

> *He assumes a bellicose attitude. Hakuren restrains him.*

HAKUREN: That's enough, Mokusuke. You are no match for him. Anyway, I am not afraid. My conscience is clear in spite of what he has said. Ofuji and Mokusuke, you two go inside and let me settle this.

MOKUSUKE: No, no, I will not go, Master. I am afraid of what might happen to you.

HAKUREN: But even a scoundrel is human and will listen to reason. Do not worry; go.

MOKUSUKE: But....

> *Hakuren cuts him short.*

HAKUREN: Come now, Ofuji, you will only be worried if you remain here listening to our conversation. Go inside with Mokusuke and keep him from intruding.

OFUJI (*concerned*): Will you be safe alone?

HAKUREN: I have a plan. Go inside and stop worrying.

OFUJI: Even so....

HAKUREN (*harshly*): I have asked you to leave. Please go.

OFUJI: Come with me, Mokusuke.

MOKUSUKE: Aye.

> *He looks at Seikichi.*

MOKUSUKE: You brazen hoodlum!

> *Music. Mokusuke, observing Hakuren
> and Seikichi, exits with Ofuji. A temple
> bell tolls. Hakuren gets up, looks cauti-
> ously into the interior through the cur-
> tained doorway. He then goes from stage
> right to stage left, and returns to sit down
> at stage center.*

HAKUREN: Seikichi, you have exposed my crime.

SEIKICHI: What?

HAKUREN: You were right. I learned by chance about the
three thousand gold pieces that Lord Yoritomo was
offering to the temple. I lost no time and stole it that
night. I made my living by stealing, and it was easy—
like getting grains of millet to stick to a wet hand. I
operated from Awa to Kazusa, from Shimōsa to
Hitachi. I specialized in temples. I was the thief called
Ōdera Shōbei.

> *He removes his hood and reveals a bushy
> head of hair—the conventional fright wig
> of an evil figure in kabuki.*

SEIKICHI (*incredulously*): I have heard about Ōdera Shōbei. So you are he!

IZAYOI: I had no idea you were a thief.

HAKUREN: I would not tell this to anyone else, but you
can steal all your life and not lay your hands on a

thousand gold pieces, let alone three thousand, in one lump sum. After I stole it, I thought it was time for me to quit. I divided the loot among my accomplices and went straight. I opened this lending office. I charged no interest on the small sums I loaned to people in distress, and they all speak well of me in this area. I have become so honest that nothing can tempt me. No one suspects, and my sleep has never once been troubled. But you cannot escape the judgment of heaven. If it had been anyone else but you, I would have denied the accusation and stuck to it. But you—the famous Seikichi—exposed me. My back was up against the wall, and I have told you everything. But walls have ears, and I cannot dawdle about here. I will leave this locality and turn thief once more. Having told you this much, I must tell you that of the three thousand gold pieces, I have only three hundred left. I will give you all of it. Spend it and enjoy life to the full. Do the things you have always wanted to do and dine well. The money is sure to slip through your fingers in the end. And give up any idea of turning honest—look at me.

> *He takes two hundred gold pieces from the chest and places them in front of Seikichi alongside the first packet. Seikichi and Izayoi exchange glances.*

HAKUREN: Here, take this. Go. If you still distrust me or think I might steal it from you, then we have come to the end of the road. Either I inform on you or you on me. Either way we must be prepared to spend the rest of our lives in prison.

SEIKICHI (*deflated*): Did you hear that, Izayoi? He has knocked the wind out of me. He is offering the last of his money. Talk about a generous spirit! Compared to his, what mean natures we have. I had come to fleece him. By making an ugly scene I expected only to get half of what I demanded of him—twenty or thirty gold pieces at the most. But his generous spirit has made me ashamed.

IZAYOI (*miserably*): Think how I feel. I don't know what others would do, but I cannot accept this money now.

SEIKICHI: You are right. Hakuren, you just said that you were going on a journey. If that is the case, money will be your first consideration. I thank you for your generosity, but I must return this to you.

> *He brings the money up to his forehead in a gesture of gratitude.*

HAKUREN: There is no need to feel that way. I will not need so much. I can make my way anywhere by pulling off a job here and there. Take it with you.

SEIKICHI: We can do the same. We will not suffer. Izayoi and I can work together. You are alone. Keep it.

HAKUREN (*proudly*): You forget who you are addressing. I have never taken money back from anybody.

SEIKICHI: Two can play at this game: who do you think I am? I will not accept your money.

HAKUREN: Don't take that attitude.

SEIKICHI (*stubbornly*): I refuse your money.

> *The two shove the packets back and forth. Izayoi steps in.*

IZAYOI: You know the saying "Get a third party to settle a dispute." Let me be the mediator. I don't expect Hakuren to take back his word or money. But let me solve the problem by accepting his gift of a hundred gold pieces and returning the rest.

HAKUREN: I will abide by your decision, Izayoi. I will accept two hundred gold pieces from you. I will not

[119]

hold you under any obligation for your hundred gold pieces.

> *He takes the two hundred gold pieces and places the packet of a hundred gold pieces in front of Seikichi.*

SEIKICHI: I do not want your kindness to come to nothing, so I will take this.

IZAYOI: Now you are satisfied. I am glad I stepped in.

SEIKICHI: But a hundred gold pieces is too much. I feel sorry for you.

HAKUREN: Are you still carrying on? Let me get you a money-belt. You don't have anything to put the money in, do you?

> *He takes a silk money-belt out of the cupboard.*

SEIKICHI: No, I need something, but I won't need that.

IZAYOI: Why don't you put it in the amulet bag you carry in your waistband?

SEIKICHI: That's an idea. I didn't give you enough credit for brains.

> *He begins to pull out from under his collar an amulet bag of saffron-yellow cotton.*

IZAYOI: Listen to him. I teach him a good thing, and he won't even thank me.

HAKUREN: That was a good idea.

SEIKICHI: This thing is stuck.

> *He yanks it out. The amulets scatter.*

IZAYOI: Oh, that's sacriligeous! You've scattered your amulets.

Izayoi gathers them up. Seikichi puts the money inside the bag. Hakuren notices the amulets.

HAKUREN (*curiously*): Tell me, Seikichi, do you belong to the Lotus Sutra sect?

SEIKICHI: Yes, my parents belonged to it.

HAKUREN: No wonder. I see one from the Lotus Sutra Temple at Nakayama to protect you from injury. Another from Komagi for the safe delivery of children. And another from Shibamata with one rice grain in it. They all seem to be from the Shimōsa region, don't they?

SEIKICHI: Yes. I was born in Gyōtoku, the son of a Shiohama fisherman. Like my parents I am a devout believer in the Lotus Sutra sect. It's a strange thing, but my religious side is partial to my native place. That is why I have so many amulets from that area.

HAKUREN: You say you are from Gyōtoku?

SEIKICHI: Yes. I lost both my parents when I was seven. Through the help of an uncle in Kamakura, I entered the priesthood at Paradise Temple to pray for their souls. When I became an acolyte, my ambition was to become a learned priest.

IZAYOI: Now that I think about it, I never learned where you were born, Hakuren.

HAKUREN: I was born in Funabashi, near Gyōtoku, and my father was a fisherman.

SEIKICHI: What a coincidence! If this were a play, we would find some evidence in our amulet bags or pill-boxes and find that we are long-lost brothers.

HAKUREN: I felt a wave of nostalgia come over me when

you mentioned Gyōtoku. What was your father's name?

SEIKICHI: Let me show you.

> *From among the amulets he picks one containing his preserved umbilical cord, and opens it.*

SEIKICHI: Here is what it says: "This envelope contains the umbilical cord of Seikichi, the son of Seiji, a fisherman at Gyōtoku in Shimōsa."

> *Hakuren takes a shot in the dark.*

HAKUREN: Did your father happen to have a crescent-shaped scar on his forehead?

SEIKICHI (*surprised*): Yes, he did. He told me he got it in a fight with the post town gang at Ōwada.

HAKUREN: Then you *are* my brother!

SEIKICHI and IZAYOI: What? What did you say?

HAKUREN: It all happened twenty years ago. I am the brother who was kidnapped when you were three. I won't take time now to show you the proof, but I am the Seitarō you must have heard about.

SEIKICHI (*astonished*): Then you are the brother my mother used to mention!

IZAYOI: This is unbelievable!

HAKUREN: To think that I would have run into Izayoi, your wife, and now into you, my own brother!

SEIKICHI: This *is* like a play!

HAKUREN: What could be more incomprehensible than the ways of this transient world? It all began with my keeping Izayoi. Now after twenty years we meet again. It's a miracle!

IZAYOI: There I was, blissfully unaware that you were my husband's brother, and blackmailing you for a packet of money.

SEIKICHI: And the seal on that packet brought to light the whereabouts of the three thousand gold pieces.

HAKUREN: It took a clever man to expose me, and who should it be but my own brother.

IZAYOI: We are as good as informers to force you to be on the run again.

SEIKICHI: It is too late for regrets. It was only a matter of time before he found himself in this predicament.

HAKUREN (*soberly*): This must be the retribution for our father's having taken so much life as a fisherman. Seikichi, you and I....

IZAYOI: ...will be caught in the Buddha's net of compassion and be saved.

SEIKICHI: But who will die first?

IZAYOI: The survivor will offer water in a bowl....

HAKUREN: ...to whoever is captured and decapitated.

SEIKICHI: Since we have a price on our heads....

HAKUREN: ...our reunion today may be our last.

IZAYOI: This may be our parting in this world.

SEIKICHI: We are in danger now and what our fate will be no one knows.

HAKUREN: In the end, our blood will rust on swords.

SEIKICHI: Hakuren!

HAKUREN: Seikichi!

SEIKICHI, HAKUREN, IZAYOI: A violent death will be ours!

> *There is a commotion, and Ofuji comes running from the interior.*

[123]

OFUJI (*excitedly*): Listen, Hakuren! Just now Mokusuke said he was going to the baths. I told him they must be closed, but he would not listen and went anyway. He acted strangely.

HAKUREN: I see. That man made some sharp observations despite his stupidity. You say he went out from the back? I wonder if he couldn't have been an agent planted in my house?

OFUJI: What was that?

SEIKICHI: If that is the case, we must be on our guard. He looked exactly like the official who read me the sentence of exile some time ago. You must lose no time making your escape.

HAKUREN: You must go first. You have Izayoi to consider.

IZAYOI: But we cannot leave you like this.

SEIKICHI: If they come now we will fight like devils, but if we are overwhelmed, we will die together.

HAKUREN: Think it over. You are still young. Run away, go!

IZAYOI: Don't think of us. Save my sister.

OFUJI (*suddenly*): I am not staying here another minute.

She prepares to go.

HAKUREN: Ofuji, where are you going?

OFUJI: I heard everything you said. I am going to the magistrate's office to turn you in.

Hakuren seizes her.

HAKUREN: You intend to give us away?

OFUJI: Yes, so that I will not be involved.

She frees herself and runs, but Seikichi

[124]

catches her. Hakuren draws his sword.

HAKUREN: You monster!

He slashes at her. Ofuji falls.

SEIKICHI: Oh, you have cut her down.

IZAYOI: My sister!

HAKUREN: I did not want her alive.

Ofuji crawls to him in pain.

OFUJI: I would have been a hindrance to you, Hakuren. Please kill me quickly before they come.

SEIKICHI: What's this? Was it your plan to be killed?

OFUJI (*painfully*): If he took me along, I would only hold him back. If I stayed I would be tortured, so I pretended I was going to inform on him so that I would die by his hands. Now he has only himself to look after. Make your escape and hide. It is not right for me to go before you, but offer a bowl of water at my grave. I will wait in the next world.

HAKUREN: You have my admiration, wife! You have done well to die by my hand. I will thank you fully when we meet again in the next world.

IZAYOI: Your death, dear sister, will be held up to all women as a shining example.

SEIKICHI: You are not one of us, but you have shown a noble resolution.

OFUJI: Oh, the more I suffer the more my attachment to life grows. Kill me quickly.

HAKUREN: I will put you out of your misery in a moment. Hail to Amida Buddha!

He stabs her in the chest. Ofuji clasps her hands and falls dead. Izayoi collapses in

[125]

> *tears. The sound of drums is heard at the head of the runway.*

HAKUREN: Get ready.

SEIKICHI: Right!

> *He bolts the gate. Izayoi picks up the money.*

IZAYOI: Here is your share.

HAKUREN: It's a nuisance, but I will take it.

> *He wraps the money in a belt and slips it under the collar of his gown. Terasawa Tōjurō the former servant Mokusuke, enters on the runway. He is dressed in a wide-bottomed split skirt, a short coat split in the back with sleeves tied up with a cord, two swords, and a headband. He carries an iron rod, a symbol of authority. He is followed by six constables dressed in black. He peers inside the gate. Two constables exit at stage right.*

HAKUREN: Izayoi, bring that brazier over here.

IZAYOI: All right.

> *She carries the small hand brazier over to him. Hakuren takes some promissory notes from the chest and puts them in the brazier. There is a burst of flames.*

SEIKICHI: What were those papers?

HAKUREN: They were notes on money I loaned. If they were found, they might cause some difficulty.

SEIKICHI: Done like a man!

> *The two constables dash forward and charge Hakuren and Seikichi.*

[126]

CONSTABLES: You are under arrest!

> *Hakuren and Seikichi dodge and parry,*
> *then scatter the constables.*
> *Hakuren whispers to Seikichi.*

SEIKICHI: We are to meet where?

HAKUREN: At the chapel of the Jizō Bodhisattva on Kobukuro Hill.

> *He says this for Tōjūrō's benefit. Then he*
> *lowers his voice.*

HAKUREN: Slip out quickly from the back.

IZAYOI: Then....

> *The two constables recover and rush the*
> *two.*

CONSTABLES: You're under arrest!

> *Hakuren and Seikichi pin them down.*

HAKUREN: Go quickly.

SEIKICHI: Right!

> *He throws the constable and exits with*
> *Izayoi. Tōjūrō breaks down the entrance*
> *and leads his men in to surround Hakuren.*

CONSTABLES: Don't move!

HAKUREN: I knew there was something strange about my servant Mokusuke. Now I see. You were an agent, eh?

Tōjūrō: Yes. I was ordered to apprehend the thief. You came under suspicion and I gained entry into this house under a ruse. You have been unmasked. Give yourself up like a man.

HAKUREN: Now that it's out in the open, it won't matter how many lives I take. I have only one life to give. On your guard!

Tōjūrō: What insolence! Move in and arrest him!

CONSTABLES: Yes, sir! Surrender!

To drum beats they rush Hakuren with raised maces. Hakuren draws his sword and scatters them. There is a fierce duel. The constables retreat into the interior of the house. Tōjūrō throws a net of mail over Hakuren. The two battle. They fall into and hold a pose in a tableau. The stage revolves and the next scene follows without a break.

VI. 2

The scene: the rear of Hakuren's house. The upper half of the rear wall of the house is fitted with a window six feet high, with a lattice of bamboo set in the plaster. Seikichi is seen protecting Izayoi with a drawn sword. She covers behind him. Constables surround them. The drum beats continue until the set comes to rest. The constables rush forward with their maces raised. Seikichi slashes away fiercely. Izayoi attacks the constables with a bamboo rake. There is a commotion and Hakuren enters from stage left with drawn sword. He joins Seikichi and hacks away. The constables run off at stage right and stage left. The three look at each other.

SEIKICHI: Is that you, Hakuren?

HAKUREN: Yes, Seikichi. It's going well.

Both wipe the blood from their swords and sheath them.

HAKUREN: We go our separate ways from here.

SEIKICHI: Right.

> *Two constables, recovering, dash toward Hakuren and Seikichi, shouting "We've got you!" But in the melee they are defeated. Seikichi and Izayoi go quickly to the runway while Hakuren takes the secondary runway opposite. The window is broken open and Tōjūrō leans out from it.*

TŌJŪRŌ: They have got away, have they?

SEIKICHI and HAKUREN: A parting shot from us!

> *They pick up stones and aim them at Tōjūrō, who ducks. The stones strike the constables, who fall. The clappers sound.*

SEIKICHI and HAKUREN: Now's the time! Come on!

> *To accelerated samisen music and the tolling of a temple bell, the two groups go down the runways. Tōjūrō gazes after them from the window. With this tableau, the curtain is drawn.*

ACT SEVEN SCENE ONE

Time: Several days later. Evening.

> *The scene: the graveyard at Muen Temple. At stage left is a shed for the preparation of corpses. At rear center is the gate leading into the cemetery. At stage right and stage left are black wooden fences. At downstage left is a well. A number of headstones are set about. A willow tree stands in the yard. Nihachi, the noodle vendor, assisted by Donshichi and Kanroku, is dragging Sukizō, the gravedigger, along. Tora is trying to pacify her father. The curtain is drawn to the tapping of the mokugyo drum.*

SUKIZŌ: Let me go! What do you want with me?

NIHACHI: What do you think? You are a kidnapper. I am taking you to the magistrate.

DONSHICHI and KANROKU: Move along!

TORA: Wait! I know how angry you are, but please forgive him.

SUKIZŌ: I plead with you.

NIHACHI: Plead all you like. I cannot forgive you. Where would you find an upstart gravedigger like you who would run off with an honest man's daughter, hide her in the shed where they wash corpses, and ruin her? Off to the magistrate's!

DORAICHI: And it's all on your account that we have been wasting our time looking for Tora.

KANROKU: To even the score, we will lodge a complaint against you and send you to prison.

DONSHICHI: Get a move on!

SUKIZŌ: Wait, wait, both of you.

> *He begins to chant comically in the puppet theater style.*

SUKIZŌ: "You are wrong to think that I enticed her. Tora came to me because she took a fancy to my chanting. You do me an injustice by accusing me of kidnapping her. See—I weep."

DONSHICHI: Don't give us any of your terrible singing. We don't want to listen to it.

KANROKU: What got into Tora to take up with this one?

TORA: Oh, you think me whimsical, do you?

> *She begins to chant.*

TORA: "I grant you there are any number of skilled narrators among professionals and amateurs. But their tunes in general are monotonously alike. Sukizō's chanting has a touch of the Buddhist service. It is unique and harmonizes more with gongs, cymbals, bronze chimes, and drums than with the samisen. Do you blame me for taking to him? Father, must I use force to convince you and push down on your head like this?"

NIHACHI: Even you make fun of me with your silly singing!

SUKIZŌ: " 'I am out of patience,' he says, and burns with rage. His bald head...."

TORA: "...turns hot like a boiling copper kettle."

NIHACHI: Stop that nonsense!

DONSHICHI: On to the magistrate's!

NIHACHI, DONSHICHI, KANROKU: March! March!

> *They seize Sukizō and start to drag him off. Funeral percussion music offstage. Sanji, with the hem of his gown tucked up, comes up the runway. He is followed by two of Hakuren's underlings who carry a burial tub draped with an unlined garment. Bringing up the rear is Doraichi, a buyer of personal effects of the dead. He carries a bamboo basket. They come to the stage and break into Nihachi's clamorous group.*

SANJI: What's this all about? It may be none of my business, but if this man has done something wrong, pardon him.

BEARER 1: You may have a reason for being angry, but remember where you are.

BEARER 2: Reconcile for the love of Buddha.

NIHACHI, DONSHICHI, KANROKU: No, no, we will not!

SUKIZŌ: "If you will not forgive me, then do your worst. I am prepared to be thrashed."

DORAICHI: Don't carry on so, Sukizō. These people are

trying to pacify them. Be patient.

SUKIZŌ: Ah, you're Doraichi—the buyer of dead men's belongings.

SANJI: I don't know what the story is, but since I'm in this, I must know.

TORA: You are most kind, but since my father will not listen to reason, it's no use.

Sanji notices Tora.

SANJI: You are Tora, aren't you?

BEARER 1: That's right. She used to be at the chief's.

SANJI: Careful! Don't mention the chief. She worked at the loan office. Now what's behind all this?

DONSHICHI: Listen. The trouble started when Tora fell in love with this gravedigger. She ran away and abandoned her father. That is why we are being so harsh with them.

SANJI: Then I don't blame her father for being so angry.

DORAICHI: But if they love each other, what is the harm?

BEARER 2: We will act as go-betweens.

SANJI, DORAICHI, BEARER 2: So forgive them.

NIHACHI: Well, girls have been known to elope, but who ever heard of a wench. . . .

BEARER 1: . . . falling in love with. . .

NIHACHI, BEARER 1: . . . a gravedigger?

DORAICHI (*soothingly*): You are upset and that is natural. But use your judgment, old man. I make the rounds of cemeteries all year to buy up personal effects of the dead. I make more money than secondhand clothes dealers with fine shop fronts. You may sneer at this man here for being a gravedigger, but I guarantee that

[134]

his job is more profitable than most. If I were you I would gladly take him for a son-in-law.

SUKIZŌ: Exactly. At the temple I get three meals a day. As for clothes, I strip them off dead men. And I have more than enough spending money from fees for digging graves and for Buddhist services.

TORA: Not only that: I can eat my fill all year 'round of the buns and rice that people offer at graves. Come to think of it, there is no other business like this one. Do you blame me for falling in love with him?

> *Tora and Sukizō recite and alternately provide vocal imitation of samisen music.*

NIHACHI (*still not convinced*): Oh, when I think of what the neighbors will say: "Has she no feelings for her father? To think that she has married a gravedigger!"

DORAICHI: Come now, gravedigger or cremator, what difference does it make? We live only to satisfy our needs. What good would money be if another cholera epidemic like the one last year should break out? Think that over and give your consent.

NIHACHI: Don't mention that epidemic. It would be terrible if another broke out.

SANJI: Anyway, this is something you can settle by talking it over. As you can see, I have a corpse to dispose of, so I cannot join you. But as mediator I will treat you to a jug of wine. Discuss the matter over a drink.

> *Sanji gives Nihachi a silver coin.*

NIHACHI: This is very kind of you, but to accept this from a total stranger....

SANJI: That's all right. We may not have met before, but I know Tora.

DONSHICHI: Come along, old man. That man's heart is in the right place. Let's go get a drink.

KANROKU: I'm ready for some wine myself.

SANJI: So am I, but I can't leave the body here. I will send my helpers along with you, so have a good time.

SUKIZŌ: Ah, Sanji, we are indebted to you for stepping into this awkward situation. "I return, I will dig an extra-deep hole for that corpse."

SANJI: That's enough nonsense.

BEARER 2: Join us later, Sanji.

SANJI: You go along, too, ragman.

DORAICHI: No, I think not. With me, food and drink take second place to money. I have to go to the shed to make my purchases.

Sanji turns to Nihachi.

SANJI: Well, old man, you know the saying, "Fall in with your children's ways in old age." Give them your blessing.

NIHACHI: Thank you for everything.

TORA: Goodbye, Sanji.

NIHACHI, DONSHICHI, KANROKU, BEARERS: Off to the wineshop....

SUKIZŌ: "...we will go."

> *To drumbeats, Sukizō, who sings a song, Tora, who vocally imitates the samisen, Nihachi, Donshichi, Kanroku, and the bearers exit stage right. With his eyes on Sanji, Doraichi exits stage left. A temple bell tolls. Offstage music is played. Sanji peers around and approaches the burial tub. He speaks in a low voice.*

[136]

SANJI: Chief. Chief. I know it's cramped in there, but it's only until evening. With circulars on you everywhere, you can't be seen in a palanquin. That's why I thought of this idea. I got two fellows just back from Kōzuke and new around here to carry you. I had them dress like day laborers, so we didn't attract attention. We will wait until nightfall and then carry you out quietly. We will travel all night as though we were on our way to a crematorium.

> *Sanji puts an ear up against the tub to listen.*

SANJI: What was that? Your brother Seikichi? I haven't heard of his being captured, so he must have escaped. I am sure he got over the mountain all right. But I hope they won't track him down on account of Izayoi. Anyway, I will get you into the shed.

> *Doraichi enters from behind.*

DORAICHI (*ominously*): If you need help, I will give you a hand.

SANJI: That is kind of you. I hate to trouble you, but will you help me?

DORAICHI: Of course.

> *They lift the tub and carry it into the shed.*

DORAICHI: That was an amazingly heavy corpse. He must have been a fine specimen.

SANJI: You're mistaken. It was a woman.

DORAICHI: It didn't feel like a woman. I wonder if that added weight could have been money?

SANJI: What?

> *He is startled.*

DORAICHI: Listen, my name is Doraichi. I buy things from

[137]

charnel houses. You wouldn't sell that to me would you?

SANJI: What do you mean? What do you want to buy?

DORAICHI: The corpse.

SANJI: What's that?

DORAICHI: A talking corpse is rare. I think I can get a good price for it.

SANJI: What's this you're saying?

DORAICHI: Of course, if you won't sell, I can't buy. But I have taken a fancy to that item. Make me a profit, and I will let you keep it.

SANJI: That's a funny way to ask for a handout. I can be generous to beggars around temples and to workers in charnel houses. They don't have to ask me. If you had said that you felt you needed a drink for helping me, I might have been generous with you, but after what you just said, I wouldn't give you three coppers.

DORAICHI: I would not have said what I did if you had a real corpse in there. I am asking you to seal my lips because the dead man in there talks. I don't need a set of scales to tell me what's in there. I knew in an instant, and I am never wrong. If you doubt me, show me the corpse.

SANJI: Well, I....

DORAICHI: You can't, can't you?

SANJI: It isn't that I don't want to, but what is the purpose of that? Here, buy yourself a drink with this.

> *He takes a silver coin out of his tobacco pouch and holds it out to Doraichi.*

DORAICHI: What, one measly silver coin? You can keep it.

> *He takes it and throws it on the ground.*

SANJI: Why, you.... I'll lose my temper in a minute.

DORAICHI: If you do, I'd like to see you do something about it.

SANJI: Don't think I won't.

> *He uproots a wooden grave marker and brandishes it. Doraichi counters with the beam of his scales. They parry. Then Doraichi dashes down the runway with Sanji in pursuit. The stage revolves. The next scene follows immediately.*

VII. 2

> *The scene: Sagobei's dwelling at the temple. The raised set is eighteen feet wide. The cell is constructed with pillars at the four corners, straw thatch on the roof, and bamboo railings. The interior walls are plastered gray, and there is a curtained doorway at stage rear. At stage left is a Buddhist altar with utensils. In front of the altar are a memorial table of plain wood, an incense burner, and flowers. At stage left the rear of the corpse shed extends out six feet. At stage right is the tombstone of a mass grave. Behind it is a thicket in which grave markers are visible. Sagobei, dressed in a gray robe and hood, applies a light at the altar. Drum beats continue until the set comes to rest.*

SAGOBEI (*sadly*): Ah, the older I get the faster a year slips away. It's like a dream. Tomorrow is the first anniversary of Motome's death at the Hundred Piles. We still don't know who killed him. Why did such a filial son

[139]

meet such an untimely death? This thought tortures me. I have tried to resign myself to his death but cannot. He entered *nirvana* a year ago in the spring. I must make some dumplings to offer to his soul.

He looks out toward stage left.

SAGOBEI: There was some commotion a while ago about Sukizō's having brought a woman into his quarters, but it has quieted down so they must have settled it. Well, I think it's time for prayers.

Sagobei sits down in front of the altar, fingers his rosary, and intones a mass. Seikichi and Izayoi come up the runway. Izayoi is carrying her child.

SEIKICHI: Izayoi, is the boy asleep?

IZAYOI: Yes, he finally dropped off.

Seikichi peers down at the child.

SEIKICHI: Poor fellow. This urchin has been taken care of by other people from the day he was born—and all because of us. Now that he is back with us, he doesn't even have a roof over his head and has to be carried around in the dead of night. It must be hard on him.

IZAYOI: I am not much help either, this being our first child. If he is going to suffer any more I would rather give him away.

SEIKICHI: When they find out who his father is, no one will take him, not even the child farms. And yet it would be too cruel to abandon him.

IZAYOI: Well, then, there's no help for it. We will take care of him as best we can.

SEIKICHI: I did not believe I would be so attached to a child.

[140]

IZAYOI: They call that paternal love.

SEIKICHI: Anyway, let's get to your father's place.

> *They come to the stage and peer inside Sagobei's cell.*

SEIKICHI: Hello! Is this Sagobei's house?

SAGOBEI: Yes, it is. Who is it?

IZAYOI: Father, it is I.

> *She pushes the gate open and enters. Sagobei is astonished.*

SAGOBEI: Daughter! And Seishin! What a surprise this is!

SEIKICHI: To tell you the truth, I am ashamed to show my face to you.

SAGOBEI: Why should you be? Here, come in, come in.

> *Seikichi and Izayoi step up into the room. Sagobei offers them tea and tobacco.*

SAGOBEI: Well, we have not seen each other in a long while, but it is good to know that you are both well.

SEIKICHI: We are relieved to see that you are well, too.

IZAYOI: I had heard that you lived here, but I could not come and see you whenever I wanted to.

SAGOBEI: Yes, I know all about it. What made both of you do the things you did? I was shocked to learn that the notorious thief called the Demon was.....

> *He catches himself in time and lowers his voice.*

SAGOBEI: ...you! What possessed you that you would change so completely in mind and appearance? Ah! You have made me the most miserable of men!

SEIKICHI: When you say that, I could crawl into a hole. Try to accept everything as having been determined in

[141]

another life and please forgive us.

SAGOBEI: Oh, don't say that. You have fallen so low on account of my daughter. Now, Izayoi, I have not seen you since you were kidnapped in the mountains. Where did they take you? What happened to you?

IZAYOI: They took me to a secret hiding place called Little Hell Valley. There I met the old woman they call the "Hag from Hell." She runs a sideshow at carnivals and buys midgets, little girls who act like birds, and cripples. Then she sells them in Kamakura. People steer clear of her. She planned to sell me right away to a brothel in a post town on the other side of the mountain. Fortunately I was pregnant and my hair was cropped short so I was worthless to her. She kept me with her hoping my hair would grow long by the time I had my child. Before I knew it I had spent six months there. I became accustomed to what had first filled me with horror. I finally gave birth to this child. As it grew, I was constantly on the lookout for a chance to escape. By some great good fortune I ran into Seikichi on the night of the festival for the mountain god. We made our way back here.

SAGOBEI: So that's what happened. You have suffered much. When they took you from me, I wanted to kill myself, but I remembered the soul I had to pray for, and I came back with a heavy heart, hoping that we would meet again. I wanted to serve the Buddha in some way and became the gravekeeper here. Now just let me see my grandson.

IZAYOI: Here, take a good look at your first grandchild.

She holds the child out. Sagobei cradles it.

SAGOBEI: Oh, what a fine child! Is it a boy or a girl?
IZAYOI: It's a boy.

[142]

SAGOBEI: That's fine. There's no doubt who his parents are. He is the living image of you, Seishin. Look, he's smiling at his grandfather. And we have only just met. What a dear fellow. Come, smile again for me.

SEIKICHI: Even such a worthless creature is lovable to a grandfather.

SAGOBEI: A grandchild is something very special. Oh! Izayoi, I think he's soaked through.

IZAYOI: Oh, that's a nice thing to do to your grandfather!
She takes the infant and changes its diaper.

SEIKICHI: We are anxious to know what happened to you. The moneylender who took Izayoi in for a while—he called himself Hakuren or some such thing—is my brother. He is also a thief. We thought they may have interrogated you about us.

SAGOBEI: They did. The day after you escaped, I was called into Tōjūrō's office. He was the manservant in Hakuren's house. He questioned me. I was shocked to hear about you. But as I could tell him nothing, he released me, and I came home.

SEIKICHI: That was fortunate, considering the situation. You will never know how much we worried, wondering about the hardships you must be facing.

SAGOBEI: You are most kind.

IZAYOI: Well, we must be thankful we can get together like this even if it's just for one night.

SEIKICHI: You are right. If we had died when we threw ourselves into the river, you would never have seen your father again.

SAGOBEI: If I had killed myself in Hakone, I would not have seen my dear grandson.

[143]

SEIKICHI: No matter how difficult things may seem, it is foolish to die.

SAGOBEI: Those words stab me in the heart. The dead are so unfortunate. Izayoi, I have a sad story to tell you: your brother is dead.

IZAYOI (*aghast*): What? Motome dead?

SAGOBEI: I have kept this from you until now, but tomorrow will be the first anniversary of his death.

IZAYOI: We only had each other. Why did you not tell me?

SAGOBEI: If he had died of a lingering illness, you would have been at his bedside at the end. But he died such a brutal death, I could not let you see him.

SEIKICHI: He did? Where did this happen?

IZAYOI: And why?

SAGOBEI: Let me tell you what happened to my poor son.

> *Samisen music with liturgical gong.*
> *Sagobei wipes away his tears.*

SAGOBEI: Last year, just before you were to be exiled, I thought I would try raising some money for you. But what could a poor man like me do? I went from one place to another. Then I ran into Motome. When I told him of my plan, he said that he would help me. He was my last chance. I waited an eternity for him. When he failed to show up, I put it down to his inability to raise the money. Then my neighbors rushed in to tell me that Motome's corpse had been found floating near the Hundred Piles. I didn't believe it. I flew there. Someone had slashed his throat and had thrown him into the river. I claimed the body and buried it. But whether he died as a result of a grudge or was killed by a thief we still do not know. He was only fourteen, just growing into manhood. Who could have killed him? If I knew who did it, I would kill him with my own bare hands. I am as bitter now as I was a year ago. I cannot forget it even in my sleep.

> *He chokes and coughs. Izayoi, weeping, rubs his back. Seikichi is anguished.*

SEIKICHI: Then it happened at the Hundred Piles, you say.

SAGOBEI: What, did you know about it?

SEIKICHI: I heard people talk about the death of a young boy there. How pitiful!

IZAYOI: Father, you once told me at Hakuren's house that you had to pray for someone's soul, and had shaved your head for that purpose. Was it for Motome? Why did you not tell me then?

SAGOBEI: I did not want to see you grieve.

> *He remembers something.*

SAGOBEI: Here's a good opportunity with Seishin right here. I would like to ask you to do something for me.

> *He brings forth the plain wooden grave marker and the inkstone box.*

SAGOBEI: I prepared the ink with the intention of having the priest inscribe this marker for me. For Motome's sake, won't you write his name on this?

> *He places the marker in front of Seikichi.*

SEIKICHI: If I were to do as you ask, it would do his soul more harm than good.

SAGOBEI: Why would that be?

SEIKICHI: It would have been a different story in the old days when I was a priest. Now people call me "the Demon." If I inscribed it, it would not serve as a

[145]

memorial or an offering. I would advise you to get the priest to do it.

SAGOBEI: I still don't see why you won't, but there's no help for it then. I will ask one of the priests to do it tomorrow.

> *He props the board against the wall. Izayoi, with the child in her arms, burns incense at the altar. Seikichi looks toward the runway.*

SEIKICHI: Who's that? I think that samurai is headed this way.

IZAYOI: I hope he's not on our trail.

SEIKICHI: We had better take no chances.

SAGOBEI: Hide in the back room for a while.

SEIKICHI: If he should be looking for us....

SAGOBEI: Slip out from the back.

SEIKICHI: Shhh!

> *Seikichi checks to see if they have been overheard. A bell tolls. Seikichi and Izayoi go inside. Sagobei looks toward the runway with a worried expression. Up the runway come Nihachi, carrying a jug of wine; and the samurai Kageyama Shigenojō, wearing a short coat with back vent, a split skirt, and two swords. He carries a lantern.*

SHIGENOJŌ: Excuse me, but is this the Muen Temple?

NIHACHI: Yes, it is.

SHIGENOJŌ: I am on my way to pay my respects at the grave of a recently-deceased man. Do you know where the graveyard is?

NIHACHI: It is there on the right, but the gravekeeper's house is over there. Inquire there.

SHIGENOJŌ: Thank you.

> *They come to the stage. Nihachi steps up into the room.*

NIHACHI: Sagobei, I have come to apologize for the ruckus we made a while ago. I brought you some wine. Have some.

SAGOBEI: You need not have worried about a thing like that.

NIHACHI: This is only a token. Take it.

SAGOBEI: I am grateful to you.

> *He takes the jug.*

SAGOBEI: Who is that with you?

NIHACHI: This gentleman told me he was looking for a particular grave.

SAGOBEI: Is that so?

> *Shigenojō enters.*

SHIGENOJŌ: I will state my business at once. Was there someone from the Ōe family who was buried here three days ago?

SAGOBEI: Yes.

SHIGENOJŌ: Will you show me his grave?

SAGOBEI: I will lead you to it.

> *Nihachi has been scrutinizing Shigenojō.*

NIHACHI: Forgive me for asking, but are you connected with the Ōe family?

SHIGENOJŌ: Yes, I am.

NIHACHI: I may be mistaken, but are you not the son of Kageyama Budayū?

SHIGENOJŌ: Yes. How did you know that?

NIHACHI: By the crest on your lantern and your resemblance to my old master. I was once a servant at your house. I was called Matasuke.

SHIGENOJŌ: Well, well, this is a surprise.

SAGOBEI: My quarters are not fit to welcome visitors, but please come in.

SHIGENOJŌ: Excuse me.

> *He steps up into the cell. He notices the memorial tablet, and sits at stage left. Nihachi sits down at stage right.*

NIHACHI: I disgraced myself while in your family's service. I have not made any calls to pay my respects since I was discharged. Is your father well?

SHIGENOJŌ: My father died last year in an accident.

NIHACHI: What? I am sorry to hear that. What was the accident?

SHIGENOJŌ: As a former retainer, you are entitled to know. My father chose a samurai without a master named Yaegaki Monza from Yūki in Shimōsa for my sister's husband. For reasons I cannot go into here, he killed my father and fled. Later he decided to return, goaded by his conscience, so that I could avenge my father's death. But he learned that he was also suspected of having stolen the Midorimaru, our lord's heirloom sword, which vanished the night Monza disappeared. Because of the theft he was ordered to disembowel himself. His last words to me on his deathbed were that it was a bitter pill to die disgraced. It is true that he was my enemy. But he also had been my broth-

er. That is why I have come to visit his grave at night.
I did not wish to be seen.

NIHACHI: What a turn of events this is! What you must
have gone through!

SAGOBEI: I don't mean to interrupt, but the Monza you
mentioned must be the son of Mondayū, the master of
the Yaegaki school of swordsmanship. I heard that
Monza murdered a colleague in an argument and disappeared. You say he committed suicide? That is sad
news.

SHIGENOJŌ: You knew Monza?

SAGOBEI: Yes, my wife was his wetnurse.

SHIGENOJŌ: What a strange karma!

SAGOBEI: Then the man we buried three days ago was
Monza? I had no idea it was he. I have not offered a
single invocation to his soul. Hail to Amida Buddha!

Nihachi has been thinking all this while.

NIHACHI: That's it! I remember I was going along the
back of the Yaegaki mansion with my noodles. A
young samurai about twenty-four or twenty-five came
charging through the fence with sword drawn. That
must have been Monza. Then what about the heirloom
sword? I don't think he had it.

SHIGENOJŌ: It was stolen that very night.

NIHACHI: A young man who ordered some noodles from
me that night had an unusual sword. I noticed it. He
must have been the thief!

SHIGENOJŌ: He is the man we are looking for.

NIHACHI: Could he have been "the Demon"?

SAGOBEI: Oh!

NIHACHI: We will be on the lookout for him.

SHIGENOJŌ: By the way, who is this Motome Koizuka whose name I see on that tablet?

SAGOBEI: He was my son.

SHIGENOJŌ: Then it must have been he who was given fifty gold pieces by my lord Ōe.

SAGOBEI: You say Lord Ōe gave him fifty gold pieces? Then he did get the amount after all. And it was on account of the money that he lost his life! Ah, the poor boy!

SHIGENOJŌ: With all of these unexpected developments, I have taken up some time. I would like to get to Monza's grave before it gets darker. I will make an appointment for a mass at the temple headquarters, and then I must be on my way.

SAGOBEI: Then I will lead the way.

SHIGENOJŌ: I am sorry to put you to all this trouble, but I would be lost without a guide.

NIHACHI: I will go along, too.

SAGOBEI: Yes, come along.

> *To music and the tolling of a temple bell, Shigenojō and Nihachi, who are led by Sagobei with a lantern, exit right. Sukizō the grave digger enters from stage right. He is dressed in formal attire, with a stiff winged jacket, and carries a circular of a description of Hakuren pasted on a rectangular board.*

SUKIZŌ: Sagobei! Sagobei! The magistrate's office has just sent round this official description! The chief priest told me to tell you that you are to hang it up on the pillar at the gate! He's not in. He must have gone shopping or something. I know he has nothing valuable, but even so it's careless of him to leave the door wide open.

He reads the circular.

SUKIZŌ: Let's see. This is Ōdera, Shōbei the thief who got away with the three thousand gold pieces from Paradise Temple. If he thinks he will not be caught, he is mistaken. Too many people will be on the lookout for him when we put up this circular.

He sings the next line to a jōruri tune.

SUKIZŌ: "The desire to live by stealing what does not belong to you is wicked. Heaven will not condone it."

Sagobei enters from stage right.

SAGOBEI: Ah, Sukizō, have you come on an errand?

SUKIZŌ: Yes. I am to tell you to put this up at the gate. It's a description of Ōdera Shōbei the thief. It's one more task for you, but you are to hang it up in the morning and take it in at night.

SAGOBEI: That's a nuisance. As if I did not have enough to do. I see you have your formal jacket on tonight. Singing again?

SUKIZŌ: I am going to recite the will-o'-the-wisp scene from the play *The Twenty-four Examples of Filial Piety* at my teacher's place across the way. Please come. My teacher asked you to come, too.

SAGOBEI: That's something to look forward to. I will come later.

SUKIZŌ: My friend Towadayū Ichisaku will chant the scene where Okoma, the daughter of the drygoods merchant Shirokiya is led to her execution for a murder plot. I follow him. Listen, I will give you a sample. "Lady Yaegaki sits in front of her lover's portrait. Would she have had it painted if she knew he were alive? She burns some pills in front of it."

SAGOBEI: "Pills"? You mean "incense," don't you?

SUKIZŌ: No. The pills cost twenty-four coppers, and the title of the play is *The Twenty-four Examples*. See?

SAGOBEI: Oh, what a terrible pun! Ha, ha, ha!

SUKIZŌ: "Well, I'm off. Come soon."

> *Chanting, Sukizō exits stage right.*

SAGOBEI: Ha, ha, ha! He's tone-deaf, and he loves singing. He is a fool.

> *His eyes fall on the circular.*

SAGOBEI: Ah, this is about Hakuren!

> *He looks about him.*

SAGOBEI: That it would come to this!

> *Samisen music. Seikichi and Izayoi enter. Sagobei sees them.*

SAGOBEI: You must have been uncomfortable inside. We have hardly had time to talk, what with unexpected visitors coming by.

SEIKICHI: Let's go to bed and talk the whole night through. By the way, I overheard that part about Monza. Was he the young master whom Izayoi's mother suckled?

SAGOBEI: Yes. Izayoi had an older brother who died an infant. Because his mother's breasts were full, she served as wetnurse to Monza for five years. I was sorry to hear about his suicide.

SEIKICHI: Karma is mysterious: you never know when or where our paths have crossed in the past. When I was living in Kamakura, my uncle used to tell me that my father had been a retainer to the Yaegaki family and that because he drank too much, he came to grief and became a fisherman. The more I think about it the more appalling my deeds become.

Izayoi: Then your father also served the Yaegaki? Then your father and my mother were colleagues. Isn't it amazing that their children should have married?

Sagobei: The god of marriage at Izumo is as good as a playwright to have woven such a complicated plot.

Seikichi: You are right. Speaking of plays, circulars often figure in them.

He picks up the circular and reads it.

Seikichi: My brother won't be free much longer.

Izayoi: Everything I hear or see tonight depresses me. Even in my father's house I am nervous and can't sit still.

Seikichi: That's because you haven't had a good night's sleep for so long, what with our running and hiding.

Sagobei: Tonight you may sleep here without a care in the world. I will go across the way to the singing teacher's for a recital. I have a jug of wine that you may have. I will be back by midnight. Enjoy yourselves until then. If you want to go to bed, the quilts are over there.

He points to the closet.

Izayoi: Thank you.

Sagobei: Well, then, I will be on my way.

Izayoi: Enjoy yourself.

> *Sagobei starts for the gate, stops, and turns back.*

Sagobei: Lock the door.

Seikichi: All right.

Sagobei: Now, to hear Sukizō chant.

> *Music. Sagobei exist at stage right. A bell tolls. Seikichi secures the latch on the*

[153]

> *bamboo lattice door. Izayoi puts the baby to sleep, pours the wine into a porcelain bottle, and puts it in an earthenware teapot over the fireplace to warm.*

SEIKICHI (*gloomily*): The weather doesn't look too good. I hope it won't rain tomorrow.

> *He steps up onto the platform. He sees Motome's memorial tablet.*

SEIKICHI: So he was your brother. How was I to know? Hail to Amida Buddha!

> *Izayoi puts the wine bottle, cups, and bowls of food on a tray.*

IZAYOI: Come, Seikichi, the wine is warm. Have a cup.

> *She holds out a wine cup. Seikichi picks up a bowl.*

SEIKICHI: The cup is too small. I'll have some in this bowl.

IZAYOI: Here you are. Take your time.

> *Seikichi gulps it down. He chokes and splutters.*

IZAYOI: I told you so. You can have all the wine you want, so don't gulp it down.

> *Seikichi holds out the bowl.*

SEIKICHI: Fill it up again.

IZAYOI: Do you think you should drink so much?

SEIKICHI: I'm in low spirits tonight. I need the wine to cheer me up.

> *He gulps the wine down.*

SEIKICHI: Here, why don't you have some, too?

IZAYOI: I am going to have an attack of cramps. I've felt it

[154]

coming ever since I heard about my brother's death. I won't have any tonight.

SEIKICHI: I'll have just one more.

> *He drinks another bowlful. The baby begins to cry.*

IZAYOI: Hush, hush. You have had a bad dream. Magic charm! Come and get rid of the dream!

SEIKICHI: Something must have told him about me.

IZAYOI: What did you say?

SEIKICHI: Nothing. I was wondering out loud if he had been bitten by something.

IZAYOI: He has fallen asleep again. Why don't we lie down for a while?

SEIKICHI: If you want to go to bed, you go ahead. I cannot sleep.

IZAYOI: Why not?

> *Seikichi rises and gets the memorial tablet.*

SEIKICHI: Because of what I have done to your brother.

IZAYOI: What are you saying?

> *Seikichi pauses.*

SEIKICHI: I killed him.

IZAYOI: Oh!

> *She collapses. The child begins to cry. Seikichi looks around cautiously to see whether they are being overheard. Izayoi recovers and then tends to the baby.*

SEIKICHI: When we jumped into the river last year, I could not drown. I floated and drifted to the shore. Then I heard the sounds of merrymaking in a boat. In that instant my mind involuntarily made a complete turnabout. Having been born a man, I thought, why not indulge myself and live for pleasure? Robbery was the answer. I killed your brother for his money. How was I to know that it was intended for me? No, I cannot sleep. We could not help it when we were ignorant of the facts. Now you know who I am: your sworn enemy.

IZAYOI: You, my brother's murderer? And fate has brought us together.

She is horror-stricken. The baby cries.

IZAYOI: Oh, don't cry, don't cry.

She rocks the child.

SEIKICHI: Can I make you understand the agony I felt when your father said that his anger has only grown more intense over the year? Then came worse news: because I stole the sword from the Ōe family, the son of your mother's master and my father's had to die. Now my own brother is being hunted down because I unwittingly exposed him when I went to blackmail him.

IZAYOI: But we didn't know any of this. It is too late for us to do anything about it now. Don't lose courage now. If you do, you won't live to see our son grow up.

SEIKICHI: I don't expect to live much longer. Those who hate me for my deeds must curse me awake or asleep. Your father said so himself. The gravedigger said that heaven will punish a thief. That was like an omen to me. So kill me and avenge your brother. Then let your father take his vengeance by offering my head to Monza and your brother.

He places his short sword in front of Izayoi.

IZAYOI (*desperately*): I know what is in your heart, but suppose you should die now—who would have one kind word to say about you? People will only laugh at you.

[156]

They will say, "If he had that much concern about honor, why did he turn thief in the first place?" People call you "the Demon" now. Then be a demon to the end, and leave off talking about death. It's cowardly.

She rocks the child in her arms.

IZAYOI: Hush, hush.

SEIKICHI: What you say doesn't change anything: I am still a fugitive from justice. Supposing I decided to live: what additional sorrows will I cause your father to suffer? What more remorse will I have to feel? The only way I can atone is by dying. Turn yourself into a demon, Izayoi, and kill your brother's murderer.

He shoves the sword in Izayoi's direction. Izayoi pushes it aside.

IZAYOI: Don't be ridiculous! You say we are enemies, but when we became husband and wife it was for two or three worlds in the future. How can you expect me to kill you?

The baby cries.

IZAYOI: Hush, don't cry. See how stubborn your father is. He says things to make me suffer. Well, Seikichi, if you insist on a killing, I must die first. I slept with your brother. True, I was ignorant of his relationship to you; but even so I must die, and I have known this for a long time. Only the thought of this child has prevented me from killing myself before this. He would have to be brought up by others. If you have any pity for me, please don't say such things to me.

Seikichi expresses pity for the child and Izayoi.

SEIKICHI: I know how you feel. My love for the child makes me realize only too well your father's anger. My son has made me appreciate what it means to be a father. But there is no reason for me to live. If I do not die by your hands I will by mine. Raise our child and think of him as me.

IZAYOI: Do you think I would survive you? I will go first. Raise this child for me.

> *She places the infant in front of Seikichi and picks up the sword. Seikichi stops her.*

SEIKICHI: Stop this folly! How can I bring him up?

IZAYOI: It is only right for a boy to be with his father.

> *The child cries loudly.*

SEIKICHI: Ah, poor boy! Don't cry.

> *Izayoi unsheaths the sword.*

IZAYOI: Now...quickly.

SEIKICHI: Stop! Look out! Let go!

IZAYOI: No, no! Let me die!

> *Izayoi attempts to stab herself. Seikichi and Izayoi struggle for possession of the sword. Seikichi accidentally slashes Izayoi deeply in the shoulder. She falls. Seikichi is aghast.*

SEIKICHI: Oh! My hand swerved!

IZAYOI (*gasping with pain*): I'm glad! I will go first.

SEIKICHI: You have acted rashly.

> *Music, with sound effects of chirping insects.*

IZAYOI: Listen: if you died and I were left behind, think of the miserable fate that would be mine. I know it is unfilial of me to cause my father sorrow not once but twice. But can I save my father from suffering? Even if I lived, they would only arrest me in the end. I would

[158]

rather die here in my father's house. This is much less unfilial. Save yourself and bring this child up yourself. That is all I ask.

SEIKICHI: Izayoi, nothing you have said convinces me that I should not be the first to die. For my son I have nothing but pity. But I do not expect to live much longer for the crimes that I have committed. I will follow you.

IZAYOI: If that is how you feel, then kill our child, too.

SEIKICHI: I've had that in mind. We will take him along with us. He will only be another burden on his grand-father.

IZAYOI: Looking back, I can only wish that we had drown-ed.

SEIKICHI: We would have been spared these sorrows. It was only because we were saved that...

IZAYOI: ...we took a crooked course and committed countless evil deeds.

SEIKICHI: There was no escape for us: our day of reckon-ing was coming. And here it is: a year to the day for the law of cause and effect to catch up with us.

IZAYOI: My brother died an untimely death.

SEIKICHI: And today, on the eve of the anniversary of his death....

IZAYOI: ...we also die, as it was fixed in another life.

SEIKICHI, IZAYOI: How brief our lives will have been!

The infant cries.

SEIKICHI: Don't cry! Dont't cry!

He pats the child.

SEIKICHI: I must leave an explanation of our deaths. Put up with the pain just a while longer and wait for me.

He gazes at the child.

SEIKICHI: Ah, cry your heart out! Death will soon come to still your voice.

IZAYOI: Oh, the pain! Give me some water.

SEIKICHI: But that would be fatal. Well, death is not far away. Here is a cup of water to mark our parting in this world.

He dips water from a bucket.

SEIKICHI: Drink this, and cut your ties from this world with no regrets.

IZAYOI: I am happy to do so.

She clutches the ladle, drinks deeply, and falls into a coma. Seikichi brings his lips to her ear.

SEIKICHI: Izayoi, listen: I will soon follow you.

Izayoi revives.

IZAYOI: Where is the boy?

SEIKICHI: Here he is. Here he is.

He brings the child up to her.

IZAYOI: Ah, I can no longer see him clearly.

She gropes for the child's face, grimaces with pain, and then falls dead. Seikichi crumples, and patting the child, weeps. A voice is heard from the singing teacher's house across the street.

ANNOUNCER: Your attention please! We begin the recital with the scene from the play *The Love of Okoma* in which Okoma is led to the execution grounds at Suzugamori.

The narrator onstage begins.

[160]

NARRATOR: "The execution grounds at Suzugamori have long been notorious: those who go there meet death. The grounds are enclosed by a fence of fresh bamboo. Unsheathed lances stand in glittering array. The horrible and fearful tortures of hell await the criminal in this world."

> *Seikichi picks up the child and puts him to sleep. He conceals Izayoi's body behind a two-leaf screen.*

SEIKICHI: What ill luck! The chanting next door is about a girl being led to her death. I thought I would suffer a criminal's death, like her. But I will die on mats in a house, not led around in public on horseback and then executed. But what about this child? He forfeits his life as though he were an accomplice. My son, it was your misfortune to have had criminals for your parents. Now you must die by the sword. Before I do, though, I must leave a note for Sagobei.

> *He picks up the circular.*

SEIKICHI: I will rip the circular off and use the board to write on. It won't take long.

NARRATOR: "Okoma's father is blinded, as all fathers are, with love for his child, and cannot resign himself."

> *Seikichi brings up the inkstone box, picks up the writing brush, looks at the child with sorrow, tears off the paper, and begins to write.*

NARRATOR: "Blinded with tears, he comes to the execution grounds, as though in a trance, as though in a dream."

> *Seikichi finishes his note. He takes a rosary from the lintel and puts it around his neck. He places the placard where the*

> *rosary had been, signifying that it is to be placed over his grave.*

SEIKICHI: When Sagobei reads this, I know he will forgive me. And Izayoi will ask forgiveness of Monza for me.

> *The child whimpers. Seikichi picks it up.*

SEIKICHI: I have never heard my son cry like this before. Surely his guardian deity must have spoken to him.

NARRATOR: "Today is the day of separation between parents and child in this world. They have come for their last farewell."

> *Seikichi presses his cheek against the child's and caresses his head.*

SEIKICHI: I have no desire to kill you. You have all your life ahead of you. But what will people say of you after our deaths when grandfather will look after you? "Look, that is the son of the thief 'Demon' Seikichi. What is in store for him?" That is why I am going to kill you. You are not a year old. But you are my son. Be brave. Go to the Western Paradise of Amida bravely, not crying like a coward.

NARRATOR: "They saw the bamboo enclosure and the terrifying unsheathed lances. 'Is our child to be killed by those?' they cried, and their hearts were crushed."

> *Seikichi picks up the child and is about to stab him, but his courage fails. He throws the sword aside and looks at the child.*

SEIKICHI: He laughs. He doesn't know how close he is to death. He melts my heart.

NARRATOR: "Only an implacable karma can explain the fate of our child: we petted her and denied her nothing. Yet here she is—a criminal about to be executed."

SEIKICHI: Those lines fill me with remorse for the many

lives I have taken, beginning with Motome's. Now I can appreciate the sorrow of the parents of my victims. I have no wish to kill my son, my own flesh and blood.

NARRATOR: "The father babbles, 'Condemn me to hell, Amida, but show some mercy to my daughter and save her.'"

Seikichi fondles the infant.

SEIKICHI: I will leave you in Sagobei's care.

NARRATOR: " 'This way, this way,' Okoma's father says to his wife, and leads her away from the crowds to comfort her."

Seikichi puts the sleeping child down. He breathes a sigh of relief.

SEIKICHI: I yearn to die, but I am drawn to my son and he detains me from my journey to the shades.

NARRATOR: "It was due to thwarted desire that the wretched and irreconcilable business of love and obligations arose. It is for love that Okoma is now so cruelly bound by cords. A river of tears flows from her downcast eyes. Sadder than a lamb on its way to the slaughter-house, she has resigned herself to her fate. Weak and weeping, she is led through the streets."

Seikichi places an incense burner and a vase on a table of plain wood. He sheds the clothing on the upper half of his body, wraps all but the point of the short sword with a towel, and prepares to disembowel himself.

SEIKICHI: If things can only be undone. But that is impossible. Having been a thief....

NARRATOR: "...the end is pitiful. The tortures of the

Mountain of Swords in hell await the criminal in this world."

> *Seikichi thrusts the blade into his belly and crumples over the sword.*

NARRATOR: "To be garroted, to be subjected to miserable shame—all this has been determined by karma."

> *Seikichi is in agony.*

NARRATOR: "Farewell to my love to whom I am pledged for two worlds. Farewell to my parents: our ties are only for this world."

> *Seikichi drags himself to the screen and looks at the concealed Izayoi.*

NARRATOR: "She peers through the openings in the fence but cannot make out her parents. Her eyes are swollen with weeping."

> *Seikichi looks at Izayoi and the child in anguish.*

NARRATOR: "At that very moment, the parents push aside the crowds and cling to the bamboo fence."

> *Shōbei Ōdera, alias Hakuren, breaks through the wainscoting of the shed and enters. Sagobei enters from stage right. They go up to Seikichi.*

HAKUREN (*horror-stricken*): You have been too hasty, Seikichi.

SAGOBEI: What is the reason for this....

HAKUREN, SAGOBEI: ...suicide?

SEIKICHI: You will find it in that confession.

HAKUREN: What? A confession?

SAGOBEI: That must be it.

He points to the placard. Hakuren reads it.

HAKUREN: "The confession of Seikichi, known as 'the Demon,' a drifter and thief from Gyōtoku in Shimōsa. When I was exiled for having broken the priest's vow of chastity by frequenting the pleasure quarters, I strong-armed my brother-in-law, taking him for a stranger, and accidentally killed him while robbing him of fifty gold pieces which were intended for me. Later, I broke into the Ōe mansion and made away with the heirloom sword the Midorimaru, and caused suspicion to fall upon my father's former master Yaegaki Monza. Still later, I was guilty of exposing my brother's identity and crimes. In Izayoi's eyes, I am her enemy. Death is the only atonement. My crimes have been without number and all have had tragic consequences. Now is the time for me to show repentance and to atone to society with my life. I am a commoner, but I will die like a samurai by drawing a sword across my belly from the left ribs to the right. Bury me where I deserve to be buried: in the potter's field." You have acted out of repentence then?

SAGOBEI: There was no need for that.

HAKUREN: You were too hasty.

NARRATOR: "The father and mother cling to each other and weep. Okoma lifts up her face."

SEIKICHI: Father, I am to blame for the deaths of Motome and Izayoi. I know how you feel, but I hope you will forgive me now.

NARRATOR: "At these words Okoma's mother is overcome, and falls into a paroxysm of grief."

Sagobei peers over the screen.

SAGOBEI (*wailing*): Oh, what miserable figures you are!

[165]

Will your death bring Motome back to life? Why did you not decide to conceal the fact that you had killed him and, with repentance in your heart, pray for the repose of his soul? The two persons I looked to as my support in my old age precede me in death. I am sore at heart when I think that I will survive you, to be pointed at behind my back as a man born under an unlucky star. Oh, why did you have to do this?

SEIKICHI: Ah, you have every reason to grieve, father, but...

NARRATOR: "...you need not weep. Think of me as having been doomed in some previous existence to be your enemy in this world. This will lighten my burden in the land of the dead."

SEIKICHI: I have only one request to make: bring this orphan up and teach him to be an honest man.

Seikichi draws out the amulet bag.

SEIKICHI: Of the hundred gold pieces in here, fifty belong to Motome; the rest is to be used for the boy.

Sagobei picks up the child.

SAGOBEI: Don't worry about my grandson. I will raise him to be a good man.

HAKUREN: I had not counted on being at my brother's deathbed. But this is the end of my luck. I am wanted in every corner of the country. Every day might be my last. If you have something more to tell me, Seikichi, do so now.

SEIKICHI: Only one thing more: after you have decapitated me, place my head at that altar.

HAKUREN: I will follow your orders.

SEIKICHI: And father, give this sword to Kageyama so that he may clear Monza.

SAGOBEI: I will see to that.

SEIKICHI: Now my conscience is clear. Let me see my son once more.

NARRATOR: "Recalling the innocence of their child, the parents weep and wail. Their cries are as loud as the waves that crash on the shore."

> *Sagobei brings the infant to Seikichi, who caresses it. Hakuren and Sagobei burst into tears. There is a commotion and Sanji enters from stage right. He is dressed as an outcast. A cord ties up his sleeves and the hem of his garment is tucked under his sash. The two bearers, also dressed like pariahs, accompany him. They carry bamboo spears.*

SANJI: We've been looking for you, chief.

HAKUREN: Sanji! And my men! What has happened?

SANJI: The scavenger got very insistent about you, so we had to run him through.

BEARER 1: Bad news travels swiftly they say.

BEARER 2: Rumors about you are spreading. We made these bamboo spears....

SANJI, BEARERS: ...to make a stand here. That's why we came.

HAKUREN: Then I cannot mark time here.

SEIKICHI: Sever my head quickly.

HAKUREN: I will.

SEIKICHI: Father, the sword to Kageyama....

SAGOBEI: Rest assured.

> *Sagobei wipes the blood from the sword*

[167]

> *and slips it into the scabbard. Shigenojō comes running in from stage left.*

SHIGENOJŌ: I will save you the trouble of coming to me. I will claim the sword.

SAGOBEI: Here you are, sir.

> *He holds it out. Shigenojō takes it and inspects it.*

SHIGENOJŌ: Ah! It is the Midorimaru. Now Monza's honor is restored. I am much obliged to you.

HAKUREN: Now to the task of putting an end to my brother's suffering.

> *He takes his sword and stands behind Seikichi.*

SANJI: Then this is...

SEIKICHI: ...our parting in this world.

SAGOBEI: May your life in the afterworld be peaceful.

> *Sagobei brings out a gong. He strikes it. Shigenojō sits on a rock at stage left. The two bearers stand at stage right. Sanji stands at stage rear with a bucket of water. When Hakuren draws his sword, Sanji pours water over it. Enduring great pain, Seikichi straightens up.*

HAKUREN: They say that a man capable of great evil is also capable of much good.

SHIGENOJŌ: This death would do credit to a samurai.

SEIKICHI: Place my head...

HAKUREN: ...on the altar. It will be done.

SEIKICHI: Then I am ready.

> *Hakuren swings up his sword. Seikichi*

> *picks up the small table by its legs and lowers his head on it. On this cue, the clappers sound.*

SEIKICHI: Offer my head....

> *Sagobei beats the gong and intones a prayer. A temple bell tolls. The curtain is drawn. There is a shout from Hakuren as he brings his sword down. This is followed by drumbeats, and the next scene is played without pause.*

VII. 3

> *The scene: the front gate of Muen Temple. At stage left is a large crossbarred gate at the base of which is a smaller stoop-gate. Near it is the watchman's shack. At stage right and left are sections of a mud wall. At the side of the shack is a large barrel to catch rainwater. Two palanquins with their side blinds pulled down are at stage right and left. Two carriers stand by. The curtain is drawn to the beating of drums.*

CARRIER 1: Say mate, what happened to the other two, Hachi and Gon?

CARRIER 2: I don't know. They went off to get some straw sandals, but they must be drinking somewhere.

CARRIER 1: I'll bet.

> *He turns toward the palanquin.*

CARRIER 1: Sirs, I am going to get our partners. I must ask you to wait awhile. Come on mate, let's go look for them.

CARRIER 2: They cause us more trouble....

[169]

> *They exit at left. Hakuren's two bearers come through the stoopgate with the burial tub.*

BEARER 1: Well, let's get up into the hills through Koshigoe.

BEARER 2: It's pitch black tonight. Just right for our purposes.

BEARER 1: Let's get to Nagoshi as quickly as possible.

BEARER 2: Right!

> *Four constables, dressed in black, enter from stage right and left.*

CONSTABLE 1: Halt!

> *He rushes the bearers brandishing an iron mace.*

BEARER 1: What's the meaning of this?

CONSTABLE 2: We know the man in the tub is Ōdera Shōbei.

BEARER 2: If that's the case....

> *He counterattacks with his pole. They duel. The temple drum continues. The bearers flee down the runway. The constables lift up the tub and exit in pursuit. A bell tolls. Hakuren appears through the stoopgate. He wears a gray robe, a monk's black habit, a hat of woven bamboo. He carries a lantern inscribed with the characters "Muen Temple." He looks down the runway.*

HAKUREN: There I was, hidden in a tub and pretending to be a corpse. But the bottom fell out of that ruse. I would have been caught, trussed up, and thrown into prison if Sanji had not offered to take my place. I have escaped being buried. Now, to escape.

> *A bell tolls. The blinds of the palanquins are flung up revealing two constables in each. They are dressed in black. They peer out at Hakuren. Hakuren sees them. He starts and then blows out the light. The constables close in on him.*

CONSTABLES: You're under arrest!

> *Hakuren throws the hat off and duels with them. They take hold of Hakuren and pin him down; but he throws them off. The monk's habit falls away. He goes down the runway. From the curtained entrance at the head of the runway four constables come to challenge Hakuren. He retreats slowly back to the stage. The second group of constables joins the first. Hakuren stands them off. The men climb up the watchman's shack and leap down from the roof; they hide behind the palanquins. The constables eventually flee down the runway.*

HAKUREN: I am at the end of my rope. I will die here like a man.

> *He prepares to rip open his belly. Sagobei dashes out from the gate with the child in his arms. He stops Hakuren.*

SAGOBEI: Wait, Hakuren!

HAKUREN: Why did you stop me, Sagobei?

SAGOBEI: For the sake of this lad. I am old. My days are numbered. When I die, who can he look to? Only you.

[171]

HAKUREN: You are right. This boy is my only kin.

SAGOBEI: Then live, do not die, and see to this child.

HAKUREN: But this place is surrounded. What can I do?

SAGOBEI: Go to the rear of the temple....

HAKUREN: ...to the charnel house, then cut across the brothel....

SAGOBEI: That's right! Quickly!

HAKUREN: Now to make my getaway.

> *Four constables enter and surround him.*

CONSTABLES: You're under arrest!

HAKUREN: Hah! I'll make you dance first!

> *Hakuren stands at stage center; Sagobei stands at stage right; the constables hold a pose at stage left. The curtain is drawn on this tableau.*